WITHDRAWN

STAFFORD LIBRARY
COLUMBIA COLLEGE
COLUMBIA, MO 65216

A Confucian Notebook

❖ Wisdom of the East Series ❖

A Confucian Notebook

by Edward Herbert

with a foreword by Arthur Waley

Charles E. Tuttle Company
Boston • Rutland, Vermont • Tokyo

Published in the United States in 1992 by
Charles E. Tuttle Company, Inc. of
Rutland, Vermont & Tokyo, Japan with editorial offices
at 77 Central Street, Boston, Massachusetts 02109.

Editorial Note © 1992 Charles E. Tuttle Company, Inc.

For reproduction rights, contact the publisher.

Library of Congress Catalog Card Number 91-78170

ISBN 0-8048-1793-6

This is a facsimile edition of the work originally published in London by John Murray in 1950.

PRINTED IN THE UNITED STATES

TO
JOHN BLUET DENMAN
IN GRATITUDE FOR ENCOURAGEMENT
AND GOOD COUNSEL

EDITORIAL NOTE

WHEN the Wisdom of the East Series first appeared in the early part of this century, it introduced the rich heritage of Eastern thought to Western readers. Spanning time and place from ancient Egypt to Imperial Japan, it carries the words of Buddha, Confucius, Lao Tzu, Muhammad, and other great spiritual leaders. Today, in our time of increased tension between East and West, it is again important to publish these classics of Eastern philosophy, religion, and poetry. In doing so, we hope The Wisdom of the East Series will serve as a bridge of understanding between cultures, and continue to emulate the words of its founding editor, J. L. Cranmer-Byng:

> *[I] desire above all things that these books shall be the ambassadors of good-will between East and West, [and] hope that they will contribute to a fuller knowledge of the great cultural heritage of the East.*

FOREWORD

In writing this book Mr. Herbert has performed a task of a kind that is apt to be neglected in England. There is need for what the French call "œuvres de vulgarisation". They need not be written by scholars, but this does not mean (as has too often been assumed here) that they must be unscholarly. That an educated Frenchman to-day generally knows something about the history and culture of the Far East is largely due to the popularizing work of René Grousset. We have suffered through not having comparable writers—that is to say, well-informed summarizers of specialist knowledge, ready to act as middlemen between the scholar and the public. Mr. Herbert's small book seems to me to be a step towards filling this gap.

ARTHUR WALEY.

CONTENTS

	PAGE
FOREWORD	vii
PREFACE	xi
TABLE OF NAMES AND DATES	xiii

NOTES:

I.	Pageant of Pre-history	1
II.	Biographical Kaleidoscope	4
III.	Book X of the *Analects*	7
IV.	Chuang Tzǔ and Confucius	9
V.	The Unmoved Mind	11
VI.	The " Change " in Confucius	13
VII.	Beloved Disciple	15
VIII.	The Label and the Contents	17
IX.	The " Genuineness " of Tzǔ Ssǔ	19
X.	The Inaction of Shun	21
XI.	Way of the Measuring Square	23
XII.	Doctrine of *Jên*	26
XIII.	The Wind and the Grass	29
XIV.	Fallibility of the Yellow Emperor	32
XV.	The Secret Self	35
XVI.	Confessions of Confucius	37
XVII.	The Praying of Confucius	39
XVIII.	The Old and the Blind	41
XIX.	Exaltation of the Awry	43
XX.	Confucius and the Creatures	45
XXI.	Taoist Menagerie	47
XXII.	The Infant's Heart	49
XXIII.	Taoism and the Infant	52
XXIV.	Taoist Touches in *Mencius*	54
XXV.	Mencius and Yang Chu	58
XXVI.	Mo Ti's Universal Love	61

CONTENTS

		PAGE
XXVII.	A Chapter on Music	65
XXVIII.	"The Hundred Schools"	69
XXIX.	Mohist Iconoclasm	72
XXX.	Ideas about War	75
XXXI.	The Block and the Chisel	78
XXXII.	The Two "Taos"	80
XXXIII.	The Taoism of Tzŭ Ssŭ	83
SELECTED WORKS BEARING ON CONFUCIANISM		85
INDEX		87

The Chinese characters in the design on the cover of this volume are those for the four Confucian virtues signalized by Mencius as the Great Four—*Jên* (kindly sympathy), *I* (justice), *Li* (good form) and *Chih* (wisdom).

PREFACE

THERE have been many introductions to Confucianism on conventional lines, in which can be found details of the lives of the Master and his successors, with accounts of his teaching and the literature of the School. The pages that follow represent an attempt to give, not a description, but an impression of Confucianism by selecting certain facets of it, which have a special significance or interest, and bringing them each, as it were, to a point or focus. In this way it is hoped, perhaps with more precision than by the conventional method, to convey to the ordinary reader enough of the general sense and setting of Confucianism to make a systematic study of it seem worth while.

It is long since the author was last in China, and his personal memories of her people have now grown dim. But the findings of her philosophers, like the flowers called everlastings, have the quality of agelessness about them, and if he has succeeded in communicating anything of this quality by these " Notes ", the work of compiling them will not have been wasted.

E. H.

TABLE OF NAMES AND DATES

SCHOOL	PHILOSOPHERS	WORKS OF THE SCHOOL
CONFUCIAN	K'UNG FU-TZŬ (CONFUCIUS): 551–479 B.C. "The Master" TSĒNG SHĒN (TSĒNG TZŬ): dates unknown. Scholar-disciple of Confucius. Traditionally connected with authorship of *Great Learning* and *Book of Filial Piety* K'UNG CHI (TZŬ SSŬ): born about 490 B.C. Grandson of Confucius. Traditionally connected with authorship of *Doctrine of the Mean* and *Great Learning* MĒNG TZŬ (MENCIUS): 372–289 B.C. "The Second Sage" HSÜN CH'ING (HSÜN TZŬ): died about 235 B.C.	THE FIVE CLASSICS:— *Book of History* *Book of Poetry* *Book of Rites* *Book of Changes* *Spring and Autumn (Annals of Lu)* THE FOUR BOOKS:— *Confucian Analects* *Great Learning* *Doctrine of the Mean* *Book of Mencius* *Book of Filial Piety* *Book of Hsün Tzŭ*
TAOIST	LAO TAN (LAO TZŬ): traditional birth-date 604 B.C. Reputed author of *Tao Tê Ching* CHUANG CHOU (CHUANG TZŬ): died about 275 B.C. LIEH YÜ-K'OU (LIEH TZŬ): (?) 4th century B.C. Identity and connection with *Book of Lieh Tzŭ* obscure YANG CHU: near contemporary of Mencius. Representative of Individualism LIU AN (HUAI-NAN TZŬ): died 122 B.C. Exponent of Taoism with admixture of Confucian ideas	*Tao Tê Ching* *Book of Chuang Tzŭ* *Book of Lieh Tzŭ* *Book of Lieh Tzŭ*, Chap. VII: philosophy of Yang Chu *Book of Huai-nan Tzŭ*
MOHIST	MO TI (MO TZŬ): about 480–400 B.C.	*Book of Mo Tzŭ*
LEGALIST	HAN FEI (HAN FEI TZŬ): died 233 B.C. Representative of Realism with Taoist affinities	*Book of Han Fei Tzŭ*
SOPHIST	HUI SHIH (HUI TZŬ): contemporary of Chuang Tzŭ KUNG-SUN LUNG: early 3rd century B.C. Disciple of Hui Tzŭ	*Book of Kung-sun Lung*

I. PAGEANT OF PRE-HISTORY

It is impossible to dip far into the pages of the little library of Confucian orthodoxy without becoming conscious of a background, which must have been very vivid to the authors or compilers, of grandiose figures of rulers and statesmen associated with prominent events in a remote past. Historically they are the shadowiest of personages, some of them being hardly more than names; but the Confucian moralists were generally content to accept tradition and legend as history, and in the Four Books there are constant allusions to the moral perfections of the wise ones among these " ancients " and the iniquities of the villains. Like faint shapes in a faded tapestry the individuals composing this ghostly company project themselves into and colour the philosophical writings, where they are introduced at frequent intervals to illustrate or justify particular doctrines. They are an imposing array including, as they do, Yao, sage-emperor of the pre-dynastic period; his successor Shun, praised by Confucius for his grave and gracious presence as a ruler; Yü the Great, the flood-controller and founder of the Hsia dynasty, noted for his frugal ways and filial piety; Chieh, the last monarch of that line, a by-word for tyranny and sadistic cruelty; T'ang, the " Completer " or " Perfecter ", with whom the Shang-Yin dynasty began; Chou, Yin's last king, a monster of the type of Chieh; Wên, master of the civic arts, and Wu, of the art of war, joint founders of the dynasty of Chou; and the Duke of Chou, regent after Wu's death, the many-gifted counsellor of whom Confucius " was wont to dream ". Confucianism saw, or thought it saw, in the heroes of this group perfect exponents of the ideals which it proclaimed; perhaps, as some of its rivals hinted,[1] it saw there only what it wished to see, for the heroic ages however "golden" must have had in them much that was still barbaric.

Taoism, too, had its parade of ancients, but the characters are different and the setting less circumstantial. In its diminutive "bible", the *Tao Tê Ching*, there are no place-names and no names of people; the appeal to antiquity takes the form of citing collectively "those of old", who are held up as patterns of Taoist virtue. These nebulous folk are invoked in the same way in the *Chuang Tzŭ* and *Lieh Tzŭ Books*, where named worthies supposedly anterior even to Yao and Shun appear as well—the Yellow Emperor, for instance, the mythical ancestor and primal overlord of Taoism.[2]

It was no coincidence that Confucianism and Taoism, so far apart from each other in direction and range, should have both drawn on pre-history for their inspiration; resort to the national origins was common to all the great schools of philosophy in the classical era. Thus, in the writings ascribed to Mo Tzŭ, where the central theme is universal love, much play is made with T'ang, Wên, Wu and the special favourite of Mohism, Yü, who are represented as practitioners of that kind of love. Again, in the fragment embodied in the *Lieh Tzŭ Book* containing the theories of Yang Chu, the argument for self-perfection by careful cultivation of the senses is backed by references to

[1] For example, the Taoist "Chuang Tzŭ", who taunted the Confucians and Mohists with the contrary uses made by them of their common models, Yao and Shun.

[2] The word "Taoism" is used in the present volume to denote the system of philosophy (if indeed such insubstantial theorizings can properly be called a system) represented by the three classics here mentioned. It excludes "Taoism" in the sense of the religion (with a ritual, a priesthood and even a papacy) which supplanted the philosophy and eventually became a synonym for superstition and imposture.

" ancients ", whose alleged scheme of living was exactly this.

The explanation of these techniques lies no doubt mainly in the sense of continuity with bygone days and ways, that was so strong in old China. A contributory factor must have been the vagueness of the pre-history on which they turned—a convenient vagueness which enabled a philosopher, however eccentric his trend of thought, to make his own selection of ancients and then, without risk of serious challenge, to remould it nearer to his heart's desire.

II. BIOGRAPHICAL KALEIDOSCOPE

IF anyone, who is approaching the study of Confucianism for the first time, should hope to find a clear and convincing portrait of its founder in the ancient literature, he is likely to be disappointed and a little bewildered. It is not that information about the life and personality of Confucius is lacking; on the contrary it is abundant, though scattered and of uneven value. Nor is it that the material is vaguely presented, for a characteristic of the literature is its simple directness. The shortcomings of the portraiture are due to the fact that the focus, as it were, is constantly changing, so that instead of a single image there are several, overrunning one another until at times the real Confucius seems lost in the blurred outlines. There is a clue, however, in the emphases placed respectively by the ancient writers on Confucius as a man, as a philosopher and as a saint or "sage".

An example of the first of these emphases is provided by Ssŭ-ma Ch'ien's account of Confucius, which dates from about 100 B.C. and is the basis of all subsequent lives of him. Ssŭ-ma Ch'ien's preoccupation was history, and the figure that moves and moralizes in his pages, though drawn from tradition with its fringes of legend, is essentially that of a historical person. This Confucius is pre-eminently a man of action, responsive to swiftly marching events; at the same time he is a man of culture, an authority on poetry, history, ritual and music. Many "sayings of the Master" embodied in the narrative serve to illustrate the principles of his teaching, but an appraisement of the man rather than of the philosopher was Ssŭ-ma Ch'ien's concern as a historian, and he was careful to include such details as the holding by Confucius of high state offices, and even to note that his stature was that of a giant.

In the *Analects*, as the title implies,[1] the philosophy is the important thing, and while some of the " sayings " have a setting of incident, the biographical element is on the whole slight. Apart from the meticulous " attitudes " of Book X,[2] the connection of which with Confucius is uncertain, there are few personal details about him ; in particular, there is no mention of the high offices referred to by Ssŭ-ma Ch'ien. But the impression of Confucius as a philosopher, which emerges from the loosely assorted chapters, is anything but slight and has real human interest, for it shows him in intimate contact with men, from princes down to the humblest of pupils, dispensing advice and delivering judgments on moral topics through the medium of familiar talk. Incidentally this talk throws up some striking portraits of his immediate disciples, two or three of whom (Tzŭ Lu, for instance) stand out as living personalities. It is hardly to be supposed that the utterances of Confucius in this work represent his actual words,[3] but there is a consistency of tone throughout them and in sense and substance they are no doubt genuine enough.

The third emphasis (on Confucius as a saint or " sage ") is exemplified in the canonical *Doctrine of the Mean*, at the point in this truly philosophical work where the climax of the argument is reached—of the arguments rather, for the train of thought is broken at intervals, suggesting a composite authorship. This climax follows an examination of the quality of

[1] The native title (*Lun Yü*), that is, of which a truer translation than Dr. Legge's " Analects " is " Conversations " or " Discussions ".

[2] See Note III.

[3] The symmetry and polish of certain of the sayings alone preclude this supposition, so far as they at any rate are concerned.

genuineness in nature and the acquisition of this quality by man,[1] and relates to the stage at which aspiration becomes attainment in the person of the saint or "sage". Confucius is here introduced as a transmitter of the moral heritage of the sage-kings of the past, but the image of him fades and tends to disappear in a glowing rhapsody on the perfectly genuine man. This ideal figure of god-like proportions, possessed of the most exalted wisdom and of all moral excellence, is no longer human; he is in fact ranked as a "partner of Heaven", thus taking his place as a power of nature alongside the other two powers, namely, Heaven and Earth. If this was really meant for a description of Confucius, it is difficult to reconcile it with an earlier passage in the same book, where the Master is quoted as confessing his personal failure to achieve even the "Way of a Gentleman"; a possible inconsistency which, among others, throws doubt on the confident assertion of tradition that the *Doctrine of the Mean* was the product of one hand—that of Tzŭ Ssŭ, Confucius' grandson.

It is not to be imagined that the three emphases are mutually exclusive in a particular work; on the contrary, they meet and mingle with a seeming capriciousness. Thus in the *Analects* Confucius is extolled in certain sayings of the disciples as if he were a saint, and Ssŭ-ma Ch'ien's biography of him ends on an adulatory note in the same sense.

---

[1] This is the *ch'êng* motif (see Note IX), which conveyed to Dr. Legge the idea of "sincerity", "simplicity" or "singleness of soul". Among various alternative renderings of it, in relation to Heaven and man respectively, are the "being true" and "growing true" of L. A. Lyall and King Chien-Kün, and the "being real" and "coming-to-be-real" of E. R. Hughes.

III. BOOK X OF THE "ANALECTS"

It is not uncommon to find as frontispieces to books about Confucius and his system pictorial representations of the Master, which are described as " portraits " of him ; but however closely these adhere to the traditional details as to his personal appearance, it is doubtful whether they really offer more than a conventional " portrait of a gentleman " of the Confucian type. A somewhat similar suspicion attaches to the material of the tenth book of the *Analects*, which purports to portray the bearing and behaviour of Confucius in private and official routine, and was accepted as a genuine likeness of him until the impact of critical inquiry shook this belief.

The other nineteen books of the *Analects* are essentially conversational in form, and the difference of literary method in the tenth could hardly escape the notice of the most casual reader. It is almost as though the compilers of the *Analects* had paused half-way in their work to insert an illustration—a portrait-study of the Master as a man, to balance and complete the main study of him as a teacher. But the internal evidence of Book X [1] suggests that it was put together independently ; it is a question, moreover, whether the figure depicted was originally intended to be that of Confucius. The older English translators of the *Analects* (Legge, Jennings and Soothill, for example) seem not to have doubted that it was ; but in Dr. Waley's version Book X appears as a ritual accretion having no biographical significance.

Whether the book is biographical or not, the fact remains that it was included in the *Analects*, and presumably those who

[1] For instance, the use of designations other than the familiar " The Master ".

so included it meant it to be taken as equally authoritative, and of equal value for morals, as the rest of the books. Essentially, what it has to offer is a mode of living patterned by ritual, expressed as the practice of a particular individual in various domestic and public situations. The ritual management of his food and dress by this individual is described in detail, but the chief emphasis is on his "attitudes" (set motions, gestures and other theatricalities) at functions or ceremonies of the Court. It would be wrong, however, to identify these attitudes with a rigid formalism, for the reverential spirit is manifest in many passages of Book X, particularly in those which deal with ritual actions matched to state solemnities.

Elsewhere in the *Analects* Confucius stresses the importance of ritual as a modulating influence, which makes shapely and comely the moral life in the same way as the concomitant of ritual, music ; but he handles the subject broadly, as a principle, without going into its practical application. In Book X the principle is exhibited in actual working.

IV. CHUANG TZŬ AND CONFUCIUS

AMONG the multifarious biographical details embedded in the ancient records, which must be discarded in arriving at any assessment of the real Confucius, are the anecdotes and remarks about him that occur at intervals throughout the collection of Taoist writings known as the *Chuang Tzŭ Book*. There is a strong controversial element in all the early classics of Taoism, and the main target of attack was naturally the greatest of the rival philosophies, that of Confucius. What is not natural is to find the Master presented in the *Chuang Tzŭ Book* with a seeming irresponsibility and wilful disregard of verisimilitude; a phenomenon which is the more surprising when the high level of intellectual achievement in the book as a whole is taken into account.

In the group of so-called " inner " chapters (the first to the seventh) Confucius is made to appear as an advocate of distinctively Taoist ideas; the idea, for instance, of " fasting of the mind ", that is, emptying the mind or freeing it from all mundane desires, so that only Tao can occupy it. Words are put into his mouth expressive of praise for the " holy cripples " of Taoism, though at the same time he is censured for alleged striving after the Taoist bugbear of personal fame. One passage even shows him as approving the abandonment (by his favourite disciple) of his own philosophy in favour of Taoism—the shedding of the " intentional virtues " of the former (with their adjuncts of ritual and music) to make room for the " natural virtue " of the latter.

Despite the confusion and unreality of the portraiture, the Confucius of the " inner " chapters is a dignified figure, whose sayings have an air of authority; he is seldom the subject of a disparaging statement, and generally the attitude towards him is one of tolerance and the respect due to a person of importance. But in the later chapters [1] the treatment of him is less complimentary; he is exhibited repeatedly as a failure or a fraud (though often still as an exponent of Taoism) and is handled with varying degrees of hostility from simple faultfinding to abuse and ridicule. This hostility is a feature of several imaginary meetings with the Taoist sage, Lao Tzŭ, where Confucius arrives as a suppliant for advice, but is usually worsted in the argument that ensues and finally retires crushed or becomes a convert to the doctrines of " the dragon ", as he calls Lao Tzŭ. There are other conversion incidents, equally unreal, which end in Confucius forsaking his books to practise quietism in his home, or withdrawing as a Taoist hermit to the wilds to consort there with the beasts and birds [2]; and, as if this were not improbable enough, he is quoted in one passage as rebuking his own followers (whom he couples with those of Mo Tzŭ) for engaging in philosophical disputes instead of governing themselves by Taoist passivity.

It is not clear whether this falsification of the mind and character of Confucius was deliberate, or whether it took shape unconsciously in the strange flowering of Chuang Tzŭ's fancy. What is certain is that there can have been little foundation in biographical fact for these antics of a Confucian marionette dancing on a Taoist string to a Taoist tune.

[1] Apart from the thirty-third and last (see Note XXVIII), which stands in a category by itself.
[2] The sort of life which, according to the *Analects*, he expressly repudiated for himself. See Note XX.

V. THE UNMOVED MIND

OF the all too few passages in the *Analects* that purport to be sayings of Confucius about himself, one of the most striking is that in which he marks off in time-stages, beginning at age fifteen and ending at seventy, his progress towards the attainment of the philosophic mind. With its packing of a mental and spiritual autobiography into the compass of half a dozen brief phrases, this passage is a particularly good example of the compression and terseness which characterize the *Analects* as a whole. And one of the half-dozen phrases—" At forty I no longer had doubts "—is worthy of note in relation to an utterance that fell from other lips at a later time; from those of Mencius, the " Second Sage ", who, according to the book that bears his name, said : " At forty I had achieved the unmoved mind."

The discourse addressed to a disciple, in which these words of Mencius occur, includes some comments of great philosophical interest on the meaning of the " unmoved mind ". The subject was a difficult one and his explanation of it appears obscure, but the secret of the unmoved mind is seen to lie in a certain way of managing two constituent elements in man. The first of these is the will, with its controlling power; the second, a vital force or principle—*ch'i* (breath, vapour or passion-nature)—which invests the body and charges it with living energy. The *ch'i* is subordinate to the will, and this relationship must be strictly preserved; neither element should be allowed to disturb the other, as each is liable to do, and the will therefore should not repress the *ch'i*. On its side the *ch'i* must be cultivated, though always under the captaincy of the will; and by cultivation is meant a fostering, not a forcing, of its natural growth.[1] In his own case, Mencius declares, he had learnt this art and practised it, and in referring to his *ch'i* he calls it " vast " ; presumably by the age of forty he had acquired a mastery of the art, for the " unmoved mind " would seem to be nothing else than the established mind resulting from a proper management (under the will) of *ch'i*.[2]

The ethical significance of all this is that the *ch'i* is linked, and even placed on a level, with the exalted principle of Right, and is stated to grow from a gathering of righteous acts. It is also matched with the mighty principle of " The Way ". It is not surprising, therefore, that Mencius should describe it as vast, sublime and rock-like ; indeed he goes so far as to say that, if well enough tended, it takes the whole world in its grasp.

[1] This is illustrated by the story of the man of Sung, who pulled (and uprooted) the growing shoots with the intention of encouraging their growth.

[2] Rather curiously, he says that the unmoved mind is not hard to achieve, and that the philosopher Kao Tzŭ, who saw things differently, achieved it at an earlier age than he did. But he could not agree, except in part, to Kao Tzŭ's formula for the unmoved mind.

VI. THE "CHANGE" IN CONFUCIUS

A CURIOUS instance in the *Chuang Tzŭ Book* of the constant tilting at things Confucian, in which the Taoist author (or authors) seems to have indulged with special relish, is the account given in the twenty-seventh essay of a change in the opinions of Confucius, which is stated to have taken place in his sixtieth year. The context is a general disquisition on the subject of right and wrong, and when the case of Confucius is brought in, he is represented as having at sixty reversed his own previous standards and even as having renounced his life-long pursuit of moral knowledge.[1] In the twenty-fifth essay a famous minister—a friend of the Master and a Confucian "gentleman"—is declared to have undergone a similar experience and (oddly enough) at the same age.[2]

The author's purpose in citing these cases was evidently to demonstrate by actual examples the instability and impermanence of standards of morality. In Taoist theory it was a grave mistake to call anything right or wrong in an absolute sense, for rightness or wrongness (so it was argued) are relative qualities and vary according to circumstances and the point of view. Any fixed standard of right and wrong must, therefore, be artificial and illusory; and the more fixed standards there are, the more serious the mischief becomes. There is no independent authority capable of deciding between them, and the result is

[1] In the thirty-first essay he is seen, at sixty-nine, on the verge of conversion to Taoism, eagerly seeking and humbly receiving instruction from an aged fisherman-recluse—one of the elusive "men of the wilds", whose mysterious appearances are a feature of Taoist literature.

[2] This was Ch'ü Po Yü, an official of Wei, whose character Confucius praises in the *Analects*.

that the Tao is lost in a warfare of words between rival schools of morality. If it could be shown that an honoured member of a school, or better still the leader himself, had come at a ripe age to realize the fatuity and futility of his moral judgments, this would be a good point to make for Taoist propaganda.

But many of the references to Confucius in the *Chuang Tzŭ Book* are obviously fanciful, and the picture of him going back at sixty on all that he had thought worth while and fought for may well be a distortion, if not a pure invention. There is no evidence in the traditional details about him of a crisis of this sort; and while the records indicate a growing sense, in his later years, of the failure of his mission, they suggest no other " change " than the substitution of a life of quiet study for the stress of reforming effort. Nor is the alleged volte-face borne out by his own account of the stages in his mental pilgrimage [1]; on the contrary, that account implies a continuous advance along one road from youth to threescore years and ten (and after).

[1] See Note V.

VII. BELOVED DISCIPLE

It is impossible to be sure of the size of the group of persons that surrounded Confucius as disciples or more or less loosely attached adherents. But the interesting thing is not whether the "outer circle" numbered three thousand odd, as Ssŭ-ma Ch'ien, the Master's biographer, averred; or the "inner circle" some threescore and ten, which is the traditional figure and represented, according to Ssŭ-ma, those who were "masters of the polite arts". It is that in a few, a very few, cases the references in the records to intimates of the Master contain the strokes and touches of a living portraiture, so that certain individuals—Tzŭ Lu especially—appear, not as conventional disciples, but as real human beings with their graces and imperfections.

In the case of Yen Hui the portrait that emerges, particularly from the *Analects*,[1] is tantalizingly slight and only partially explains the admiration, amounting almost to awe, felt by Confucius for this saint-like disciple, who lived in poverty and died early. This admiration seems to have been directed mainly to three special qualities in Yen Hui:—a passion for "learning" (that is, acquiring moral knowledge), an exceptional teachability (or capacity for absorbing moral lessons without effort) and a power of perseverance in virtue (which Hui was able to sustain "for three months on end" without once lapsing from it). What all these qualities come to is really an innate apprehension of goodness, and in this probably lay the secret of the young

[1] The references to Yen Hui (like those to Confucius) in the Taoist classics are largely fanciful. Thus, in the *Chuang Tzŭ Book*, he is shown as a practitioner of the Taoist technique of "sitting with an empty mind".

man's "nearness to perfection"—of his superiority, in the eyes of Confucius, to the other disciples and even to Confucius himself.

For in classifying different kinds of knowledge Confucius gave the intuitive perception of moral truth the highest place, though he was careful to disclaim such knowledge for himself, explaining that his own was of the secondary kind that comes, not instantaneously, but from patient study and analysis of what is good. It may not be without significance, too, that the author of the *Doctrine of the Mean*, who quotes Confucius as praising Yen Hui for his choice of the Mean and adherence to the good, was himself an advocate of the primacy of intuition in the moral sphere and made it a characteristic of the "sage" or saint. It was thus a very exalted thing that Confucius found to admire in his favourite disciple : the same thing that Mencius in later years developed as the "mind of infancy",[1] the counterpart of the natural virtue of Taoism.

It is recorded that, when Yen Hui died, Confucius broke down in such a way as to shock or at least surprise some of those about him, and his reaction generally to the tragic event suggests that he not only admired Hui, but was genuinely fond of him. The nature of the pupil's personal feelings towards the Master can only be surmised. That he profoundly respected his teaching method is clear from a famous passage in the *Analects*, where he also eulogizes the teaching itself as a mysterious summit, towering and remote, which draws men on yet baffles their attempts to reach it.

[1] See Note XXII.

VIII. THE LABEL AND THE CONTENTS

In contrast to the Taoists, who objected on principle to anything that tended to delimit or define, the Confucians rejoiced in a Doctrine of Names and gave much thought to "adjusting the name to the reality". But the well-known dictum about this ascribed to Confucius in the *Analects* is a disputed one,[1] and there is no reliable evidence of his having personally enunciated the doctrine in its general form.

In that form it meant that the label attached to anything, and the contents, should faithfully correspond; in other words, that the name or term should represent the thing as it really was. Any false description, or failure of anything to come up to (or if a living thing to live up to) its proper name, upset the balance of the equation and violated the principle of genuineness, thus bringing confusion and, if carried far enough, chaos into the world's affairs.

This recognition of the reality of a thing, of its genuine as distinct from its apparent nature, might seem to imply a consciousness in Confucian minds of the metaphysical absolute. But they were not concerned for purposes of this doctrine with the problem of reality as such; and while, in insisting on the "correction of names", they sought to give the abstract principle of genuineness a practical application, they were primarily interested, not in all names, but only in the social designations ("prince", "minister", "father", "son" and so on).

[1] As regards both its genuineness and its meaning. Some scholars have judged it to be a late interpolation; others have held that what was to be "adjusted" was not the name but the written character. The dictum appears also, with a historical setting, in Ssŭ-ma Ch'ien's biography of Confucius.

There are indications in the *Analects*, apart from the disputed passage, that the mind of Confucius moved on these lines. Associating with each designation what he held to be appropriate qualities (with the name "son", for example, filial piety), he would not have it used of anyone failing to display those qualities, at least until the latter so improved himself as to merit the designation.[1] In thus "adjusting the name to the reality" over the whole field of human relationships, his expectation was clearly that of those who developed the doctrine after him: namely, to make of language an effective instrument of government, by means of which the professions of individuals or groups could be tested, and their performances viewed in a true perspective, as a basis or starting-point for reform.

The most important designation in the Master's catalogue was, of course, the "gentleman"—that compound of Confucian virtues, the description of whose "attitudes" occupies so prominent a position in the *Analects*. It is noteworthy that Confucius disclaimed the name of "gentleman" for himself, apparently considering that the reality in his own case corresponded only to the name of "man of letters".

[1] In one passage he is quoted as exclaiming scornfully against a certain kind of drinking vessel, which had kept its name although its form had been altered. The allusion was to the disjointed governmental conditions of his time.

There is evidence in the *Book of Mencius* of that sage also having participated in the discussion of 'names". (See "Notes on Mencius" Arthur Waley in Asia Major, Vol. I., Pt. I. New Series, 1949, p. 106).

IX. THE "GENUINENESS" OF TZŬ SSŬ

THE moral attributes that were ingredients in the composition of a Confucian "gentleman" were many and various, and it was open to individual doctors of the school to deploy them for purposes of instruction in any way they pleased. In the arrangement of Confucius—the Confucius of the *Analects*—the apex of the pyramid of virtues was *jên*[1]; in the case of Mencius also it was *jên*, with *i* however in close association[1]; but Tzŭ Ssŭ (if he, Confucius' grandson, in fact wrote the *Doctrine of the Mean*) gave the primacy in qualities of character to *ch'êng*, that is, to genuineness (usually translated "sincerity") or being one's real self.

The remarkable thing about Tzŭ Ssŭ is not the emphasis that he placed on *ch'êng*, nor the exuberant praise, which at times ran riot, that he bestowed upon it. It is so rare, so very rare, in actual life to find a man or woman who is truly *ch'êng*—the good companion, utterly sincere, who never in any circumstances will "let one down", the fine edge of whose manners no amount of familiarity will ever dull. And if, as seems probable, Tzŭ Ssŭ had found in his grandfather just such a person, it is not surprising that the discovery should have moved him to elevate *ch'êng* to a position of paramountcy among the virtues. About the method of acquiring this quality, and the symptoms and signs of it in action, he has nothing particularly striking or original to say; it is to be got by hard, unflagging efforts to choose and cling to what he calls "the good", and the possessor of it is master of himself, and is also capable in a mysterious way of causing others to be masters of themselves, and of forwarding in general the work of "heaven and earth". It is when he

[1] See Note XII.

comes to treat of the nature of *ch'êng*—to describe it in the terms available to him, which were barely adequate for the expression of his thought—that Tzŭ Ssŭ is interesting and important and ahead of his time.

For, penetrating more deeply into the subject than any of his predecessors or contemporaries, he posits *ch'êng* as an ultimate, an absolute thing. But it is more than a mere idea, it is a reality of the universe: a cosmic principle, like the principle of " Heaven " (the natural and moral order in the knowable world). The alpha and omega of existence, it is all-completing; in the human sphere it is the means by which the individual self is completed (that is, perfected in *jên*, the highest virtue), and in the sub-human that by which things generally are completed (that is, perfected in " knowledge "). *Ch'êng*, therefore, is vast in its potentialities; and equating it—in an entirely novel way—with time and three-dimensional space, Tzŭ Ssŭ ascribes to it the attributes of continuous duration and indefinite extent, and identifies it with Infinitude itself.

But if genuineness or " sincerity " meant all this, what hope had man in his homely, creeping course on earth of reaching or even approaching it? Tzŭ Ssŭ's answer to the question is clear and precise. *Ch'êng* is actually to be reached only by the sage, but it is the business of the ordinary man, essential to his development as a moral being, to seek and strive with all his faculties to *approach* it. It is true that the path of this approach, though convergent, is endless—asymptotic, like the mathematical straight line that draws ever nearer to a curve yet never meets it. There is no need for dismay on that account, however, for the path is rich in compensation and promise. " Let a man proceed in this way," says Tzŭ Ssŭ, " and though dull, he will surely become intelligent; though weak, he will surely become strong."

X. THE INACTION OF SHUN

ON the political side of the Confucian ethic, as it is developed in the *Analects*, a good deal of attention is given to the functions and obligations of the head of a government. Thus, as to character, it is expected of him that he should cultivate and display in his own person (and thereby mould to his likeness the impressionable " people ") the great Confucian virtues of kindliness, justice, filial piety and so on. Again, it is incumbent on him, in his administration, to see that only men of moral worth are appointed to positions in the public service ; and further to see, in the field of manners, that the prescriptions of ritual are fully and faithfully carried out.

One would imagine that these responsibilities, along with numerous others that are laid to him, would have kept a head of government constantly active, and certain sayings of Confucius in the *Analects* refer to the anxieties of rulers and the arduous nature of their task. It is at first sight surprising, therefore, to find Confucius in the same work eulogizing the semi-mythical Shun, a model emperor of the Golden Age, as one who merely adjusted himself with gravity and reverence on his throne and " did nothing else ". In a further allusion to this " effortless ruling " or " government by inaction " Confucius links with the name of Shun that of his successor, the Great Yü, the story of whose engineering feats suggests a man of action, if ever there was one.

These apparently un-Confucian utterances would seem to be accounted for by the difference in capacity between the ordinary ruler, who is still in process of attaining to the goal of government, and the " sage " with his transcendent power of personality, who has actually reached it. That goal is in both cases the same—the tranquillization of the empire or state, so that the entire social organism, with its apparatus of immemorial custom, is at harmony with itself under the transforming influence of its overlord. But when the overlord is a sage, good government is spontaneous and all exertion is eliminated from it; in other words, its operation is "inactive", in the same way (to use a homely illustration [1]) as a spinning top is said to be "asleep" when at the maximum intensity of its action.

The idea of spontaneity that thus emerges almost casually in the *Analects* [2] is of special interest as representing a point of contact with the school of Taoism. Though utterly at variance in most respects as were the rival systems, at the elevated level of " the sage " there was the common ground of this idea between them. But in Confucianism the doctrine of " activity in stillness " was only touched on; in Taoism, on the other hand, it was central and fundamental.

[1] Given by Dr. Isabella Mears in the notes to her translation of the *Tao Tê Ching*.

[2] As it does elsewhere in the Four Books; for instance, in the *Doctrine of the Mean*, where the principle of genuineness is extolled for its " doing nothing, yet achieving all ". See Note XXXIII.

XI. WAY OF THE MEASURING SQUARE

The treatment, which is commonly given in Western accounts of Confucian ethics to expressions of the Golden Rule in the Four Books, is apt to obscure the fact that in only one of those books, the *Great Learning*, is the Rule built, as it were, into the scheme of the ethics. In the *Analects*, where it is posited by Confucius as a life-long watchword for the moral man, it stands alone in distinguished isolation, being neither co-ordinated with other maxims nor worked into a connected argument. The *Book of Mencius*, rather surprisingly, contains no reference to the Rule at all. In the *Doctrine of the Mean*, where it figures as one of a number of sayings ascribed to the Master, it seems to be introduced mainly as a peg on which to hang a confession by the latter of his personal failure to hit the mark in any of the Rule's four directions.[1]

The central theme of the *Great Learning*, which is more of a planned treatise than the other three books, is the supremacy of moral power (*tê*) and the steps which a prospective ruler must take (and which the ancient sage-kings took) to acquire this power and "abide in it". From the study of phenomena as his starting-point this personage must proceed to enlarge his moral knowledge to the utmost extent; he must next secure that his purposes are genuine,[2] and then that his mind is freed from emotional disturbances. Having gone thus far he is qualified to undertake the momentous task of "cultivating the self"; but individual perfection is not enough, and he has the

---

[1] That is, failure to treat his father, his prince, his elder brother and his friend, as he would wish to be treated if in their places.

[2] See Note XV.

duty also of establishing the principles of goodness in his own family. For the next step—an extension of this to the State—little effort is needed; on the basis that moral goodness is infectious (a belief strongly held by the Confucians) the influence of the one well-ordered family will spread to other families, until all society is permeated by it, when efficient government automatically supervenes. The prospective ruler will then be in sight of the end and consummation of his progress—the community at peace under the lordship of *tê* triumphant.

It is in connection with this last phase that the author of the *Great Learning* presents, as an instrument for the maintenance of that peace, the doctrine that the treatment which a man dislikes to receive himself he must not mete out to others. Having previously touched indirectly on the principle of reciprocity in human conduct, he here formulates it with considerable elaboration as a definite "Way" of life, using as a symbol to describe it an item in the equipment of a carpenter, the measuring square. It is a mark of development in Confucian ideas that the simple precept laid down by the Master as one for the individual disciple to follow, should be thus generalized and embodied in a curriculum of government. The "single thread running through all" his teaching (identified with reciprocity in the *Analects*) had none of the stiffness and formality attached to it in this work.

The choice of the measuring square to symbolize the Golden Rule in the *Great Learning* contrasts strongly with the disparagement of it and of its fellow-instruments (the compass, arc and plumb-line) in the philosophy of Taoism. The worker in clay or wood, as Taoists saw him, was a violator of nature, and the tools of the craftsman appear in Taoist literature as emblems of digression from the Simple Way. So in the *Chuang Tzŭ Book*, where the potter and carpenter are represented as priding themselves on their skill and attracting praise from mankind throughout the ages, the author asks: Is it natural (is it right?) for clay and wood to suffer the application of these instruments?

XII. DOCTRINE OF "JÊN"

It would seem from the *Analects* that the compilers of this work were prompted by a twofold motive in their task: a desire to demonstrate the greatness of Confucius as a moral philosopher and teacher of morals, and anxiety to give an impressive display of the qualities that went to the making of a Confucian "gentleman". In each of the books (except the tenth, which occupies a position apart) there are "sayings" which treat of these qualities either singly or in carefully disposed groups.[1] But there is no indication anywhere of an organic relationship between the qualities, though to one of them—the virtue *jên*—a peculiar and overriding importance is attached.

Jên is stated in the *Analects* to have been one of three things about which "the Master seldom spoke". Yet references to it in sayings of his are plentiful throughout this work, and it is the leading topic of one book (the fourth). What chiefly emerges from these, however, is a steady refusal on the part of Confucius to satisfy the curiosity of disciples, who persisted in asking for a definition of *jên*. He conveyed to them that *jên* was something extraordinary, which could not easily be talked about, still less defined; at the same time he was not unwilling to enlighten them as to its manifestations—to disclose the flower, as it were, while concealing the root.

The flower of *jên* was a composite one, made up of recognizable virtues—the basic qualities of courtesy, loyalty and so on, which were the substance of the Master's teaching. But a flower (as Chuang Tzŭ predicated of a horse) is greater than the mere sum-total of its component parts, and *jên* itself, in its actuality, not only embraced but transcended those other qualities. It was clearly a more exalted thing than "benevolence",

[1] For example, "The Five Things" (qualities) of Book XVII.

which in certain contexts expresses its meaning; if it were not, Confucius could hardly have said that he had never known anyone with a real fondness for *iên*.[1] It was to be found, of course, among the sages of antiquity, but precisely what this unique faculty connoted the reader of the *Analects* is left to guess at. "A sublime generosity of soul" might perhaps describe it. It stood for virtue generally in its highest sense, rather than for a particular virtue, and belonged (like the natural goodness of the Taoists) to the sphere of intuitive, as distinct from acquired, knowledge. But if it was out of reach for ordinary men, these could at least—and should—pursue and ponder it; was there not Yen Hui, the beloved disciple, an adept in the study of *jên*, for them to imitate? There were varieties or degrees of *jên*, and any progress in its direction was a moral gain.

It is interesting to compare with this featuring of *jên* the treatment of the same subject in *Mencius*, where the virtues (that is, the major ones) are presented on an organic basis in a regular framework.[2] So clear indeed is the theory of Mencius about these, that it is not unduly simplifying it to set it out in tabular form, as follows:

Seeds of the Virtues	The Virtues	Fruits of the Virtues
Sense of pity	JÊN (kindly sympathy)	Service of parents
,, ,, shame	I (justice)	Respect for elders
,, ,, deference or respect	LI (good form)	Ordering and adorning the above two things
,, ,, right and wrong	CHIH (wisdom)	Knowing and abiding by the above two things

---

[1] Presumably he meant to except his disciples, one of whom at any rate was unquestionably a lover of *jên*. See Note VII.

[2] See Note XXII.

While the primacy of *jên* is retained in this arrangement, it is a different quality from the *jên* of the *Analects*; or rather, it is the same quality divested of its vagueness, of its mystic and transcendental character. In exhorting heads of the feudal states, as he did repeatedly, to "govern by *jên*", Mencius seems to have assumed that they understood the phrase; for he neither defined nor explained it to them, though in other contexts he plainly indicated that it meant the opposite of "governing by force". In the Mencian sense *jên* was something roughly equivalent to "kindly sympathy", but (as in the *Analects*) it was as much an attitude of mind as a quality, and terms like "benevolence", "love", "fellow-feeling" are little better than makeshifts for conveying its meaning.

A notable feature in the *schema* of Mencius is his linking to *jên* of the quality *i*, which signified "justness", "doing what is right or fitting". His idea in this apparently was that a feeling of kindness if unaccompanied by appropriate action was not enough; that right doing was the necessary complement and natural partner of good feeling, and that *jên* therefore must go hand in hand with *i*. In insisting on the marriage of these two virtues he seems at times to treat them not only as superior to, but even as subsuming, *li* and *chih*; thus, dwelling in *jên* ("man's peaceful home") and following *i* ("his true road") he declares to be "the *whole* business of a great man". But this can only have been a matter of emphasis, for in summarizing the attributes of a "gentleman" he is careful to enumerate all four virtues, which "rooted in the heart" (he goes on to say) objectify themselves and are "visible in the gentleman's looks and bearing and in the movements of his body".

XIII. THE WIND AND THE GRASS

THE maxim of Confucius recorded in the *Analects* that " to go too far is as bad as to fall short " is typical of his advocacy of the Middle Way, that is, the way of moderation in conduct and thought. And the statement in the *Book of Mencius* that " Confucius never went too far " indicates that in this he practised what he preached. It is a question, however, whether on one point of his teaching—the power of example in a ruler—he may not in fact have " gone too far ".

It is common knowledge, which history amply confirms, that the influence of example in moral affairs can, and under favourable conditions does, accomplish prodigious transformations. But is there any foundation in the facts of experience for the claims made by Confucius on behalf of this influence ? There is neither vagueness nor ambiguity in his presentation of these claims. On the principle of " adjusting the name to the reality " [1] he insists that a ruler should be in truth a ruler : the one fixed light in the centre of a host of moving lights, " the pole-star " of his people. To Chi K'ang Tzŭ, a dictator in the State of Lu, he offers three propositions on the subject. These are (*a*) that if a ruler leads in the straight course, his people will not dare to diverge from it ; (*b*) that if a ruler is not covetous, his people will not steal " though paid to do so " ; and (*c*) that if a ruler desires what is good, his people will be good. The image of " the grass bending to the wind " was well chosen by Confucius to illustrate these sequences. The doctrine, either expressed or implied, of supreme individual virtue commanding a universal docility is a frequent topic in

[1] See Note VIII.

the *Analects* and the Four Books generally; to Mencius it appealed in a special way and he proclaimed it again and again with passionate energy.

" We find the principle [that example is all but omnipotent] pervading all the Confucian philosophy . . . the subject is pushed to an extreme and represented in an extravagant manner . . . the sage of China and his followers attribute to personal example and to instruction a power which we do not find that they actually possess." This reaction of Dr. Legge's to pronouncements of the kind addressed to Chi K'ang Tzŭ was a natural one when the standpoint taken was simply that of human experience. Neither in the sage's time nor since has the admittedly wonder-working power of example worked such wonders as the Confucians claimed for it. But the charge of extravagance is apt to be misleading, for the power in its Confucian signification had a strong element of miracle in it, and the miraculous is not necessarily extravagant. To Confucius and his school the hero-saints of antiquity—Yao, Shun and the rest—were semi-divine figures endowed with a personal " essence " which was not only moral but magical. In so far as it was magical, it could achieve results which a mere moral force obviously could not—the involuntary turning of fascinated eyes on the part of an entire community towards it, the spontaneous yielding of all minds to the spell of its virtue.

The great Confucians, the Master included, looked for the coming of a True King, who should re-establish the reign of goodness and draw all China to him by the magnetism of his example.[1] The average ruler—a Chi K'ang Tzŭ—would do well to bear this tremendous possibility in mind; was it not

[1] The Taoists had a similar expectation, and in the *Lieh Tzŭ Book* there is a mysterious reference to the actual presence of a True King " in the West ".

the case (as Mencius said) that the ordinary man might become a Yao or Shun? He could at any rate, within the limits of his capacity, endeavour to be a pattern to his people, and to the extent that he succeeded the ancient magic would assuredly perform its work of transformation. It may be that some such reasoning was behind the Confucian presentation of the Doctrine of Example, and that (granted the miraculous element in it) it was not quite so exaggerated or absurd as Dr. Legge and others have supposed it to be.

XIV. FALLIBILITY OF THE YELLOW EMPEROR

In any list of "ancients" and others alleged to have attained perfection in the Taoist sense, one would expect to find the name of the remote ancestor of Taoism—Huang Ti or the Yellow Emperor. And where such a list in fact occurs in the *Chuang Tzŭ Book* (the sixth chapter), that mighty if mythical name is duly included. Elsewhere in the same book the Yellow Emperor is exhibited in a variety of situations—as a suppliant for instruction at the feet of a mysterious "mountain-man", an adept in Tao; as a practitioner and exponent of his own music, the paradoxical expression in sound of Taoist "stillness"; as an illustrator of aphorisms that appear in the *Tao Tê Ching*. But the references to him (a considerable number) are by no means uniformly complimentary, and the adverse criticism, where it occurs, is somewhat startling as applied to a Taoist "ancient". For the Yellow Emperor is charged, not once but repeatedly, with having been the first (or one of the first) to disrupt man's primal state of Pure Simplicity and Perfect Virtue.

The belief in an actual Age of Innocence at a time when the world was very young emerges strongly in the *Chuang Tzŭ Book*, where the primitive scene is described again and again, with variations, by the author (or authors).[1] It was an Age of Ignorance, in the sense that men had no such thing as conscious, objective knowledge; what they had were their instincts and intuition, the only kind of knowledge by which the mystery

[1] In the *Lieh Tzŭ Book* this paradisal state, revealed to the Yellow Emperor in a dream, is made to appear as the cause of his embracing the Tao. References to it are a feature also of the *Huai-nan Tzŭ Book*.

of Tao and its attributes could be apprehended. In ethics (as in all things else) it was an Age of Spontaneity, in which action was never planned but always natural; when no one bothered about right and wrong, yet all were good without striving to be so and practised the great virtues without being aware of them. Politically and socially it was an Age of Equality, free from distinctions of class or rank and with "birds and beasts" in the comradeship of man; free too from desire, for man's wants were minimal, being met by the products of fieldcraft and simple weaving. And as a reflection of Tao, supremely quiescent and calm, it was an Age of Tranquillity, when life ran smoothly and sweetly with the aimless yet orderly rhythm of the four seasons.

From the Taoist standpoint it was most reprehensible to have started, or have contributed to starting, the world's decline from that paradisal state; and for pressing "intentional" virtues on the world, and thereby accelerating the decline, the Confucian ancients (Yao, Shun and the rest) are severely censured in the *Chuang Tzŭ Book*. But it is just this for which the Yellow Emperor, who preceded them, is censured also; and as committed by him—a Taoist ancient—the offence was tantamount to a betrayal of Taoist truth. In addition to this public lapse on his part he was guilty (or so it would seem) of a personal failure of a serious kind; for he is represented in a curious parable as losing his "dusky pearl", his faith in Tao, and recovering it only after futile searches in the realms of knowledge, sense-perception and argument. Of the many inconsistencies in the *Chuang Tzŭ Book* there is none more glaring and difficult to account for than this presentation as a spiritual renegade of one who otherwise figures as a paragon of virtue. Perhaps the Taoists' rooted objection to names and a reputation had something to do with it; it was un-Taoistic to attract the limelight, and the Yellow Emperor was far from satisfying the test of anonymity and "leaving no trace".[1]

In contrast to this, the "great ones" of Confucianism are uniformly portrayed in the literature of that school, with a rather monotonous insistence, as impeccable. Their function in the Confucian set-up was to serve as shining models for the governors of men, and no shadow of dispraise could be allowed to impinge upon their brightness. The statement of Confucius recorded in the *Analects* that he "could find no vestige of a flaw in Yü" is typical of this indiscriminate laudation.

[1] His name too was linked, in legend or semi-legend, with certain innovations obnoxious to Taoism; for example, the invention and employment of boats and carts. This may have encouraged a critical attitude towards him.

XV. THE SECRET SELF

To judge from the *Analects*, Confucius himself was not an advocate of the practice of meditation as an aid to the good life in society; in fact, he seems to have definitely rejected it, for he is recorded as saying that he once spent a whole day without food and a whole night without sleep, in order to meditate, but that it was time wasted which would have been better employed in learning.[1] Whether this was intended to represent a personal experience is uncertain, but the lesson is clear and it is repeated elsewhere in the *Analects*; on one occasion, for instance, he spoke of thought divorced from learning as a positive danger, and again, when told that a certain official used to think thrice before acting, he remarked that twice would have been enough. But a different view from the Master's was apparently taken by the scholar-disciple Tsêng, for the latter—according to the *Analects*—said that he examined his conscience daily "on three points", to guard against self-deception in his motives and conduct.

In the *Great Learning*, the authorship of which is traditionally associated with this same Tsêng and his school, there is a brief passage on the theme that a "gentleman" should keep watch over himself when he is alone. The basic idea—which is also that of an important part of the *Doctrine of the Mean*—is the necessity for genuineness in the purposes and practices of man, and the point made in this passage is that, if his motives are not tested in private, a man is likely to deceive himself, imagining his conduct to be genuine when it is not. It would seem that

[1] That is, study of the principles of right living as laid down by the ancients.

this testing was regarded as a simple process, for no directions or hints are given as to how it is to be carried out.

The author or authors of the *Great Learning*, and Tzŭ Ssŭ (Confucius' grandson) or whoever else wrote the *Doctrine of the Mean*, were basically at one in what they thought and taught; and the opening chapter of the latter work, in which certain key-words are defined, contains the same injunction to a man to be watchful over himself in his solitude. This is here expressed as an inference from the paradox that " nothing is clearer than what is concealed, nothing more manifest than what is minute", but it is not explained in any way, nor is it related in terms of the principle of genuineness as in the *Great Learning*. It was, however, considered a sufficiently important element in the scheme of the book for Chu Hsi, the great Neo-Confucian, to mention it specially in the notes which he appended to the text.[1]

The stresses thus laid on the value of introspective study of the secret self, as distinct from learning in the Confucian sense, are interesting for two reasons: first, as showing that Confucianism in its prime had at least one instrumentality other than the sacramentals of ritual and music, and secondly, as illustrating the growth of new buds of doctrine on the parent stem under the green fingers of the cultivators of the Great Tradition.

[1] So also in the notes attached to his re-arrangement of the text of the *Great Learning*, special attention is drawn by Chu Hsi to the section of that work in which self-examination is dealt with.

XVI. CONFESSIONS OF CONFUCIUS

One gets the impression, from a perusal of the *Analects*, that Confucius was disturbed by a tendency in his disciples to set him up as a stained-glass hero to the detriment of his reputation and the effectiveness of his message. Of the recorded sayings of the disciples about him, some (particularly those of Tzŭ Kung) would certainly have been condemned by him as extravagant. That he was anxious to discourage this kind of thing seems clear from the insistence, in sayings of his, on the limited scope of his purpose and work, and the emphasis placed by him on his personal shortcomings.

He was careful to point out that the body of doctrine, which he had to communicate, was nothing new; that it was a precious gift inherited from the past; and that his special function was to hand it on intact for the benefit of his own age and posterity's. But, though only an agent, he was evidently conscious of possessing in that capacity an exceptional competence. In one of the rare instances in which he permitted himself an expression of self-praise, he claimed that in a hamlet of ten houses it would be hard to find anyone so fond as he of " learning ", by which he meant study of the ancients and their moral lore. His ambition was to be recognized as an expert in this subject and accepted as an authoritative teacher of it; he deserved (and knew it) commendation to that extent, but deprecated honours paid to him that went beyond this.

He was willing also to take credit to himself for extraordinary diligence in the prosecution of his task; and in so doing he avowed himself a plodder, whose knowledge, he frankly stated, was acquired (that is, built up by patient effort) and not spontaneous or intuitive like the knowledge of the sage. In addition he defined, or rather delimited, his personal position in the moral hierarchy, disclaiming any right to be ranked in the highest category as a " man of divine virtue " or in the next highest as a " man of *jên* ".[1] He denied, too, that he was a " possessor of wisdom ", though he was ready, he said, to hammer out any moral problem that the humblest of pupils might bring to him.

He went, it would seem, to even greater lengths in the direction of modesty and humility, for there is evidence in the Four Books of his having accused himself, not once but repeatedly, of failure to practise himself what he preached to others. The relative passages in the *Analects* suggest that he aimed to achieve at least the " Way of a Gentleman ", but that certain of the requisite qualities (that of moral courage, for instance) were lacking in him and beyond his powers of attainment. In the *Doctrine of the Mean*, where the " Way of a Gentleman " is described as a fourfold path of service,[2] he is quoted as admitting to divergences from all that path ; and it is interesting to find him thus revealed as an ordinary human being in a book which elsewhere treats of him [3] as a hero-saint.

These confessions of Confucius fit naturally in with what is otherwise known of his character, and have an authentic ring about them despite the efforts of " idealizers " (the great Chu Hsi included) to belittle their significance. It is a mark of the difference between Confucius and Mencius that the latter, for his part, made no such revelations ; less sensitive and surer of himself than the Master, he seems to have had no sense of inferiority to trouble him.

---

[1] See Note XII.

[2] Of son to father, of minister to prince, of younger to elder brother, of friend to friend.

[3] Or seems to do so. See Note II.

XVII. THE PRAYING OF CONFUCIUS

THERE has been much debating among scholars and others as to whether Confucius was personally religious.[1] The material for forming a judgment on this question (which involves a prior definition of religion) is, however, exceedingly jejune. Confucius' main preoccupation was, of course, with moral character and conduct; and the records dwell, almost wistfully, on his habit of reticence about the deeper things—the nature of man, the meaning of death and so on. Even in the *Analects* the field of survey is represented only by a few brief passages, all of them more or less enigmatic and therefore open to a variety of interpretations.

One of the least ambiguous (so far as it goes) and perhaps the most intriguing of these passages is that which depicts Confucius, at a time when he was seriously ill, discussing with a disciple the propriety of having prayers said for him. The idea of such intercession, apparently, did not commend itself to the Master, who is recorded to have closed the argument with the words: " My praying has been going on a long time." There seems to be a distinction here between formal recitations of prayer, and praying in the general sense of a lifting of the human spirit towards Something above itself. And as to the latter, the question naturally arises: what was that Something in Confucius' case?

It almost certainly could not have been Shang Ti, the supreme dispenser of moral judgments on the personal side of the Chinese Heaven; for his name is not mentioned once in the sayings ascribed to Confucius in the *Analects*, and in any case this august

[1] Dr. Legge's description of him as " unreligious rather than irreligious " seems to occupy a middle position among the conflicting opinions.

Being was more a personification than a personality. The word *t'ien* ("heaven"), on the other hand, occurs fairly often in the *Analects*, where it is used by Confucius in its established acceptation; it stands, that is, for the principle of nature (as manifested, for example, in the round of the seasons), and for the moral order as a power and an influence controlling and shaping the destinies of mankind. It was from this impersonal heaven that Confucius believed himself to have received his "commission", and it is evident that he respected it profoundly; but it may be doubted whether the all-embracing principle (as to which he asked: "Does it ever speak?") quite lent itself to the devotional intimacy implied in his reference to his long-continued praying.

One is tempted to speculate on another possibility: to associate the object of that praying with the concept of "the sage". This is not indeed made much of in the *Analects* (not nearly so much as, for example, in the *Doctrine of the Mean*), but the sage is there given the premier place in the moral hierarchy of Confucius, whose conviction that sages once lived on earth is shown by his eulogies of Yao, Shun and the Great Yü. As far superior to "the gentleman" as the latter is to "the common man", the sage is entirely free from error and towers above the world in a supremacy of virtue, which is intuitive, effortless and complete. Confucius remarked on one occasion that it had not been his lot to come in contact with a sage, but whenever he alluded to the subject of sagehood he did so with manifest reverence and awe. Is it fanciful to suppose that his steady, far-seeing eyes looked up from time to time for encouragement and strength to that ideal figure of the Perfect Man; or, again, to wonder if that same figure, at the last, was available to walk with him as a divine companion through the dark valley of disappointment and defeat?

XVIII. THE OLD AND THE BLIND

"Professor A. E. Ross has noted that the old man in China is a most imposing figure, more dignified and good to look at than the old men in the West . . . China is the one country in which the old man is made to feel at ease." So wrote Dr. Lin Yutang in *My Country and My People*.

Indications of the respect in which old age was held by the Confucian school are to be found in sundry passages of the Four Books. Thus in the *Analects* it is recorded that Confucius, when telling two of his disciples what he desired most, put first in the list of his wishes the provision of comfort for the aged. Again, in the work ascribed to his grandson, there is praise for the ancient custom of assigning a place of honour to old men at the festal table in the ceremonies of the ancestral temple. From a similar standpoint the author of the *Great Learning*, in expounding the "principle of the Measuring Square",[1] laid down as the first duty of a ruler the treatment of his old people "as the old should be treated". So also Mencius hoped to see, in the ideal conditions for which he strove, the old folk clothed in silk and fed with meat and relieved from carrying burdens on the roads.

In all four books respect for old age is expressed as an extension of the principle of filial duty, but pity for the infirmities of old age was clearly an ingredient of this respect, and the promptings of pity alone explain the references in the *Analects* to consideration for the blind. These references are in the form of personal details about Confucius, who is described as making gestures of

[1] The Golden Rule expressed negatively; that is, not treating others as one would not like to be treated oneself. See Note XI.

special deference when coming across any blind person. He is represented also as receiving (to the surprise of a disciple) a blind music-master as his guest with every mark of courtesy, guiding his footsteps and naming to him the other guests—a course of action which perhaps his own devotion to the art of music tended to make him follow the more readily.

In the hands of Mencius the emotion of pity, involved in these attitudes towards the old and the blind, came to be invested with a high philosophical significance. Believing, as he did profoundly, that human nature was essentially good, he saw manifestations of this inborn goodness in certain stirrings of the mind, of which the feeling of sympathizing pity was one. So the mind is stirred by this feeling, he said, at the sight of a child about to fall into a well. The same feeling, he went on to declare, is the beginning of the greatest of virtues, benevolence or love.[1] The subject had not previously been developed in this way, and it is to Mencius that the honour belongs of having enriched the Confucian ethic with the Doctrine of Compassion.

[1] See Notes XII and XXII.

XIX. EXALTATION OF THE AWRY

The fact that the whole movement of thought in Taoism was towards the primitive and the "uncut" accounts for the peculiar outlook of that philosophy on deformity and other physical distresses. The victims of such handicaps, so far from being objects of pity, were regarded as fortunate and in a position of privilege.

This attitude is clearly expressed in certain parables of the *Chuang Tzŭ Book*, where the doctrine of "following nature" is illustrated by the example of extraordinary trees. The argument here briefly is that the essential thing about a tree is its unimpeded existence, the spontaneous development of every part (stem, branches, foliage and so on) in accordance with its "virtue" or inborn tendency. It is better to leave a tree alone to fulfil its functions in the natural way than to cultivate it for the sake of its timber or fruit, and a tree which owing to inherent defects (such as knotted stem, twisted branches) is useless for any practical purpose, is specially blessed, for those very defects save it from interference and mutilation by man and enable it to carry out the law of its being. Though good for nothing in the eyes of the world, it has use from the point of view of Tao—the highest order of use, that is, the possession of which gives it a place of honour above all ordinary trees.

Elsewhere in the *Chuang Tzŭ Book* [1] the same lesson is taught by reference to cripples, hunchbacks and other wrecks of humanity, the description of whom in some cases is heightened by an elaboration of horrifying detail. One such miserable

[1] And also in the *Lieh Tzŭ Book*, which is in some respects similar to, and has certain matter in common with, the *Chuang Tzŭ Book*.

creature is depicted as deriving a threefold benefit from his deformity—freedom to engage in the simplest occupations, exemption from calls of the government for soldiers, and a chance to complete the natural term of his existence. Again, mutilation of the body as a punishment is represented as a stepping-stone to sagehood, in which state a dismemberment is as nothing and can be forgotten. So, too, in connection with extreme ugliness the point is made that perfection of the mind is what matters ; a goal which is obviously more susceptible of attainment if the body is not caught up in the toils of the world, as a perfect body must be. There is no room in all these anecdotes for the sentiment of compassion ; and indeed no better illustration could be found of the contrast between Confucianism and Taoism than this passionless treatment of human unfortunates by the latter.

Timber in the rough and clay in the unmoulded mass : by such symbols Taoism sought to express in language its ideal of Primitive Simplicity. In so far as the timber is wrought upon or the clay worked up, to that extent these substances suffer diminution of their respective " virtues " or proper characters ; and hence it follows that, whether of wood or clay (including human clay), the " vessel of a more ungainly shape " is nearer to Tao than the perfectly fashioned vessel.

XX. CONFUCIUS AND THE CREATURES

It is perhaps symptomatic of the depth of the cleavage between Confucianism and Taoism, that Confucius seems to have cared very little for the wild or the tame living things of nature, except of course for the mightiest of them, man. It is true that in recommending for study the ancient ballad-poetry of China, he drew attention to its mentioning of " the names of many birds, beasts, plants and trees "; but the basis of that recommendation was the moral benefit to be gained from the poetry, and its " names " from nature probably appealed to him mainly as useful items of cultural information. A more realistic hint of his attitude towards the brute creation is given by the famous " incident at the ford ", when a chance meeting with Taoist recluses prompted him to remark that what mattered to him was the reforming of men, and that " one could not consort with birds and beasts " like these recluses. In line with this detachment from actuality in the case of animals, was his reaction on a certain occasion to news that some stables had been burned down; he was anxious, the record says, for details of the human casualties, but he " did not make any inquiry about the horses ". His antiquarian researches apparently extended to the *remains* of animals, for his biographer, the historian Ssŭ-ma Ch'ien, depicts him as able to identify strange bones which were unearthed and shown to him. It is curious to find, after all this, so level-headed a person as Confucius toying with superstitions about legendary creatures; but there is evidence (in the biography and the *Analects*) of an interest on his part in the influence on his fortunes of the fabulous phoenix and dragon-horse or unicorn.

The Four Books of Confucian orthodoxy reflect generally the outlook of the Master and touch hardly at all upon organic nature below the level of man.[1] In *Mencius*, certainly, kindness to animals is advocated; but it is dealt with impersonally as an abstract principle, being graded as an inferior form of the kindly sympathy due between human beings.

[1] The tendency in Confucianism to speak of "birds and beasts" in terms which emphasize the difference of level between them and man, is illustrated by the observation in the ritual book, the *I Li*, that the former (in contradistinction to the latter, with whom the paternal relationship is paramount) "know their mothers, but not their fathers". In Taoism the tendency was in the reverse direction, and in the *Chuang Tzŭ Book* this knowing of mothers, but not fathers, is mentioned as a virtue of the people in the golden age of Primitive Simplicity.

XXI. TAOIST MENAGERIE

THE austerity of the *Tao Tê Ching* is such that the doctrine of "following nature" in it, though promulgated with intensity and force, is supported by the barest minimum of concrete illustrations. The fact is that "nature" in this work is treated as a process, not as a panorama; and when natural features and objects, animate or otherwise, are mentioned, they are brought in mainly as symbols of ideas. Thus streams and rivers, whose downward movement reflects the yielding character of water, stand for the Taoist principle of non-assertiveness; and the valley, or hollow place in the hills, represents the quality of receptivity. As to wild living creatures, the rhinoceros (or buffalo) and tiger alone are specifically named and they appear only as emblems of danger,[1] immunity from which is conferred by the power of Tao. There are one or two references to domesticated animals, but these are merely incidental.

In contrast to this, how the beasts and birds seem to riot and revel through the pages of Chuang Tzŭ! Whatever the topic of philosophical discussion—the theory of relativity, for instance—the ranges and reaches of living nature, even supernature, are drawn on for illustrations. The subjects of these are sometimes fantastic, like the linked sea and air monsters of the first chapter; and occasionally the technique of fable is used, the creatures conferring together in human fashion. But

[1] These animals also figure symbolically in certain sayings ascribed to Confucius (for example, in Ssŭ-ma Ch'ien's biography, where the Master, quoting from the ancient poetry, introduces them as types of inhabitants of the wilderness).

for the most part they are treated objectively, and in general they serve to exemplify the principle of spontaneity in Tao—the capacity of every individual thing to express itself without restraint or effort in accordance with its proper nature. At intervals and in turns throughout the book, the haired, furred, feathered and scaly tribes are evoked to testify to this freedom; thus, the pheasant of the marshes, which is free though it has to go searching for its food, is exhibited as superior to a pheasant in a cage, where it may be lavishly fed but its naturalness is curtailed.

The presentation of Taoist tenets in the collection of writings known as *Lieh Tzŭ* is assisted in much the same way by images from nature. But there is this difference that, while Chuang Tzŭ's attitude towards the brute creation is dispassionate and his interest in it largely academic, there is discernible in the *Lieh Tzŭ Book* a feeling of kinship with animals and birds and of sympathy with them for their own sakes, which is more than a mere approval of them as illustrations. This is a matter of tone and temper rather than of prescription, for it was not until several centuries later, when Buddhist influence had made itself felt, that kindness to creatures below man's level emerged as a positive precept in Taoist teaching.

XXII. THE INFANT'S HEART

A MEMBER of Confucius' " inner circle " is quoted in the *Analects* as saying that, on the subject of human nature, the Master maintained a strict reserve in communicating his views to his disciples. It appears, however, from his recorded statements that he was not wholly silent on the point, and from some of them (the one, for instance, that " uprightness is man's very life ") it is possible to deduce a faith in the fundamental goodness of man's nature. But he does not seem to have enlarged on this at all, and his avoidance of the topic, if deliberate, may have been due to his holding that history (which for him meant the tradition of the ancients) was a sufficient sanction for his moral doctrines, and that therefore there was no need to reinforce them with theorizings about human nature.

In seeking to promote the purposes of Confucius some century and a half after his death, Mencius superadded an intellectual sanction to the historical one, no doubt hoping thereby to increase the persuasiveness of the message he had to transmit. In the so-called " psychological " passages of the book that goes under his name, he treats of the nature of the mind and its workings with much subtlety and depth, though there is little attempt to prove his ideas, which he presents as findings or laws to be accepted and obeyed. Human nature (man's mind—*hsing*—that which differentiates man from the animals [1]) he regards as the soil or seed-bed of the virtues, and as such he holds it to be essentially good. The evidence of this goodness he sees in certain germinating processes of the mind, initial pulsations active from birth and common to all men, of which

[1] A vital difference, although he calls it a slight one.

he names four—the good feelings of pity, of shame, of deference or respect, and of right and wrong. And these native promptings are for him nothing less than the early shoots of the virtues, especially of the four chief virtues—*jên* (kindly sympathy), *i* (justice), *li* (good form) and *chih* (wisdom). Since all men, he seems to argue, have the seed-bed of the virtues in them and start life with the early shoots in action, it is open to all to achieve, in accordance with their individual capacities, the fair flowering of *jên* and its associates, if only they will nourish the shoots and develop them.

But he is fully alive to the hostile influences that impede and impair this work of cultivation, and in a striking allegory [1] he stresses the blighting effect on it of the impact of everyday affairs, which the night's breath and the breath of dawn may mitigate to some extent but cannot remove. It is for each man to struggle with these influences and overcome them so far as his conditions permit; if he happens to be a sage, the victory is complete and the four beginnings—the early shoots—of the virtues are brought to their fulfilment. If he is less than a sage, and yet in the struggle retains his hold on those beginnings, he will be virtuous and, it would seem, worthy to be called " great " (in the moral sense).

For, says Mencius, " he is great who has not lost the infant's heart ", and " the infant's heart " can only mean the human mind in its primitive freshness with the early shoots still green and tender in it. The owner of this mind of infancy (which is also the sage's mind) knows intuitively what is right and acts rightly without the use of thought; thus the babe-in-arms loves its parents, and the growing child respects its elder brothers, not consciously but by natural impulse. The tragedy of losing

[1] The parable of the Niu Mountain, which has a simple beauty and is a favourite of translators.

THE INFANT'S HEART

that pristine goodness, and the imperative necessity of recovering it, are the dominant themes of Mencius in the "psychological" passages; indeed he declares the whole object of man's effort in the moral sphere to be the recapture of the mind which has gone astray.

XXIII. TAOISM AND THE INFANT

It will usually be found instructive, when studying particular points of Confucian doctrine, to examine their counterparts (if any) in the opposite, yet in some ways complementary, scheme of Taoism. Such comparisons are valuable as enabling the two schemes to be viewed simultaneously in their mutual relationship.

The angle of approach to " infancy ", in the case of Mencius, was psychological ; what interested and attracted him was the child-mind—the repository (so he believed) of original goodness. In Taoism, on the other hand, the accent on infancy was physiological ; spontaneity was the all-important principle, and what better example of this could there be than the little child, organically considered ? Another important principle was " strength through weakness ", and of this also the infant was an example ; for had it not well-defined qualities of strength—its firmness of grasp, its incipient virility, the vigour and freedom from strain of its vocal expression ?

The praises of the state of infancy, which are sounded in the *Tao Tê Ching* and echoed with variations in the *Chuang Tzŭ Book*, are noteworthy for the hints which they give of practices symptomatic of the decline of Taoism. In the former work there is a curious reference to managing the vital force—the breath—so as to make it soft and pliant like a little child's ; a process which the author describes as " opening and shutting the heavenly gates " (the mouth and nostrils) in " female " (or passive) fashion. Such exercises of the breath [1] had a twofold

---

[1] In addition, there were certain exercises of the limbs ; for instance, the " bear-like " and " bird-like " antics mentioned in the fifteenth essay of the *Chuang Tzŭ Book*.

significance. In the first place, they served to produce an atrophy of the organs of sense and an "emptiness" of the mind; a condition favourable to the Taoist ideal of mystical absorption of the consciousness in the unity of Tao. In the second place, they were held to be conducive to longevity. There is a certain grossness about methods of trance and efforts to prolong the life of the body, and where these cruder elements impinge on the pure philosophy of the Taoist classics, the shadow of Taoism in decay is already apparent.

The Taoists attributed to their ancient sages and to contemporary "spirit-men" (possessors of Tao) an immunity from perils that beset the body—perils of fire and frost and flood, of horns and talons and teeth, of weapons of war. In the *Tao Tê Ching* a similar immunity, related to molestation from wild creatures, is credited to "the infant" as an embodiment of Tao.[1] But there is no certainty that these ascriptions were intended to be taken literally (that is, in a "magical" sense as in later Taoism), and perhaps the respective authors were only saying in a poetical way that the power of Tao was very wonderful indeed.

One gets glimpses in the *Chuang Tzŭ Book* of Taoist recluses, who in spite of advanced age were noticeable for still having "baby faces". The idea of "the infant", so important doctrinally, was thus manifested in the saints of Taoism for all to see.

[1] This attribute of infancy is brought out also in the *Lieh Tzŭ Book*.

XXIV. TAOIST TOUCHES IN "MENCIUS"

In his powerful advocacy of the principles of Confucius, Mencius was nothing if not outspoken ; and so far as rival systems were concerned, those of Mo Ti (universal love) and of Yang Chu (self-perfection) came in for some scathing comments from him. But he had no corresponding censure, it would seem, for the competing cult of Taoism, although its most brilliant exponent, Chuang Tzŭ, was alive and flourishing in his day. On the contrary, there are indications in the *Book of Mencius* of a not unfriendly interest in Taoism and even of borrowings, perhaps unconsciously, from it ; at any rate this work contains ideas and images which are distinctively Taoist in type, and the instances of these are too numerous for the parallelism to be accounted for by coincidence.

One such instance is to be found in the famous argument between Mencius and Kao Tzŭ, where the latter compares the process of producing *jên* and *i* from human nature to the fashioning of cups from the wood of the willow ; an analogy which Mencius rejects on the ground that cup-making from willow involves doing violence to the character of the wood, whereas no violence is done to human nature in developing the virtues from it. The reference here to something destructive in a working up of the substance of wood might have come straight from the mouth of a Taoist, although in that case the object (which was far from being Mencius' object) would have been to demonstrate the merits of Primitive Simplicity. For the creative use of raw materials Taoism normally [1] had nothing

[1] Exceptionally, there is commendation for the craftsman who " follows nature " in his work ; as, for example, in the nineteenth essay of the

but condemnation, and in the *Chuang Tzŭ Book* one essay (the ninth) is devoted to showing that manipulative processes (those, for example, of the artist or craftsman on clay, wood and jade) are damaging to the primal integrity and contrary to the special aptitudes of the things dealt with.

Kao Tzŭ follows up his analogy from cup-making with one from the behaviour of water, comparing to a stream's readiness to flow either east or west, according to the direction of the channel dug for it, human nature's proneness to good and evil alike without predilection for either. Mencius counters this by pointing to the tendency of water to flow downwards, which is natural to it but may be reversed by forcing; in like manner, he declares, the tendency of human nature is towards goodness, though external influences may deflect it towards evil. One has only to glance through the *Tao Tê Ching* to see how Taoism favoured water as a symbol; its predisposition to seek the lowest place (the downward tendency referred to by Mencius) being used repeatedly to illustrate the last and greatest of the author's " three treasures "—the quality of " not presuming to be foremost ".

The remark of Mencius in his dissertation on the " unmoved mind " [1] that he had become an adept in managing his " vast *ch'i* ", is a further indication of a link with Taoism, which, like him, attached supreme importance to the " keeping " of that vital breath. But the methods of " keeping " it—of restoring to it and maintaining without diminution its original vigour— if not entirely dissimilar in the two cases, were widely different;

Chuang Tzŭ Book, where the carver of a wonderful wooden bell-stand explains how, after inducing a state of semi-trance to give free play to his skill, he had found a forest-tree perfect in form, which inspired him with the form for his bell-stand.

[1] See Note V.

thus, in Mencius' view, the *ch'i* could only grow if constantly nourished by righteous acts, and righteousness in the Confucian sense was one of the things most obnoxious to Taoism. Again, in Taoism there was the curious accompaniment (occasionally alluded to in its early classics) of techniques for managing the physical breath to preserve the life of the body and prolong it; but there is no evidence that Mencius approved of these [1] and every reason to suppose that he would have objected to them as a " forcing " of the growth of the *ch'i*.

The statement of Mencius that for mind-development there was " nothing better than fewness of desires " is unaccompanied by any exposition of how few the desires should be, or which desires should be eliminated and in what order; but it was doubtless connected with his doctrine of the *ch'i*, and perhaps what he had in view was a pruning of that passion-nature to facilitate its cultivation under the will. The statement strongly suggests a connection with Taoist teaching on the subject of desire, though according to that teaching all the desires, not merely a majority, called for extirpation, since all tended to pre-occupy the mind and so to frustrate the great purpose of " empty-ing " it. But Taoist doctors referred with apparent indifference to " freedom from desire " and " fewness of desires ", and the modified asceticism implied by the latter corresponded to the inclinations of Mencius, who was no extremist in matters of disciplining the mind.

If Mencius seems at times to adopt a Taoist rather than a Confucian standpoint (as in praising the intuitive virtue of Shun and the effortless handling by Yü of the flood-waters), it must

[1] That they were not always approved of even by Taoists is shown by a passage in the fifteenth essay of the *Chuang Tzŭ Book*, which further intimates that in the higher Taoism longevity could be attained without such practices.

be remembered that Taoist touches occur in the recorded sayings of Confucius himself, and that parts of the work ascribed to his grandson [1] have the stamp of Taoism clearly impressed on them. It is as though the great Confucians were conscious of a certain inadequacy in their doctrinal apparatus, and, turning from ethics to speculative philosophy, found that the Taoists had something to offer in that field. The manifest influence of the latter on Mencius is perhaps explicable to some extent by the passionate interest of both in the Life of the Mind.

[1] The *Doctrine of the Mean*—see Note XXXIII.

XXV. MENCIUS AND YANG CHU

It would be interesting to have had from Mencius some sober criticism of the philosophy of Yang Chu [1] instead of a mere tirade against him, which adds nothing to what is otherwise recorded on the subject. All that emerges from this about him is that he "concentrates first and last on self and abrogates the principle of sovereignty"; the rest is a warning, purposely exaggerated, of the dire consequences to society if his theories should be adopted. It is not difficult, however, to imagine the shape that Mencius' strictures would have taken, had he chosen to develop them seriously and in detail.

He would certainly have contested with the utmost vigour Yang Chu's central recipe for self-cultivation. For what could be more menacing to his own method—a tending of the inborn shoots of goodness to produce a florescence of the Four Great Virtues [2]—than Yang's seductive call to give free play to shoots of a very different order: the promptings of the desires, as of the eye for beauty, of the ear for music, and of the mind to have its way? How ill this fitted with the injunction of Confucius to treat each faculty of the body as a servant of ritual! How contrary to all that Mencius stood for, this substitution of a sheer delight in living for the stern pursuit of moral duty!

If there was one thing in the Yang Chu set-up calculated to rouse the indignation of Mencius and provoke a spirited rebuttal from him, it was surely the attempt to dim or extinguish certain

[1] Or the Yang Chu school. It is not known how far Yang personally was responsible for the doctrines associated with his name.
[2] See Note XXII.

of the high lights of Confucian hagiology. Shun, Yü, the Duke of Chou and the Master himself : all are depicted as misguided individuals, who wore themselves out in grandiose undertakings, losing thereby the joy of life and gaining nothing but the mirage of a posthumous reputation. And—what to Mencius would have been still more galling—these honoured names are actually coupled with those of the arch-villains Chieh and Chou, to show that in death the righteous and the wicked alike revert to undifferentiated dust.

Among other matters which would have given Mencius scope to join issue with Yang Chu, were the linked topics of infancy and old age. In Yang Chu's view it was important to realize that the effective period for self-development—that is, for cultivation of the senses—in the life of man was strictly limited ; for it was necessary to deduct from the normal span (which in any case was short enough) the years of immaturity and decay, when the senses either had not yet functioned fully or had ceased to function. Thus curtly to dismiss infancy and old age as philosophical irrelevancies was to invite the disapproval of Mencius, who, reverencing human beings of all ages, had his special doctrine of " the infant's heart " and was deeply concerned for the welfare of the elderly and infirm.[1]

Yang Chu deprecated poverty and wealth on the ground that each had worries of its own, and worry of any kind was of course detrimental to pleasurable and contented living. Mencius disliked poverty as such, because it was practically impossible for people in want to attend to their manners and moral duties ; but he regarded the experience of poverty as a valuable instrument for shaping character, and in a famous passage numbered it among the prerequisites of a man with a great mission. In another passage, equally famous, he declared it to be a mark

[1] See Notes XVIII and XXII.

of the truly great man that poverty could not daunt [1] nor wealth corrupt him; and elsewhere, as if to underline the danger to morals inherent in wealth, he denounced the proud owners of luxurious establishments. While Mencius and Yang Chu were thus agreed that a middle state between poverty and wealth was the best for mankind in general, the former would not have passed unchallenged the latter's argument for this choice; in fact his comparison of the quest for creature comforts to the life of animals suggests, although he mentions no names, that he had the maxims of the sense-philosopher in mind.

In a community made up of individuals, each bent on fostering the natural life of the body with happiness as the end in view, there could be no place for sovereignty or the service of a sovereign; and Mencius was correct in charging Yang Chu with setting aside an immemorial relationship, upon which, according to Confucian ideas, good government depended. But in asserting that Yang was "all for self" and quoting, in support of this, his unwillingness "to pluck a single hair from his body for the benefit of society", he was less than just to the individualism of his rival, which indeed demanded an absolute priority for nurture of the self, but yet found room, when that demand had been met, for the exercise of compassion and kindness to the needy and distressed. On this point, if on no other, it would have been gracious in Mencius, the apostle of compassion, to have accorded Yang Chu a mark of his commendation.

---

[1] In this connection he may have been thinking of the favourite disciple of Confucius, Yen Hui, who against a background of want and squalor exhibited the highest degree of virtue.

XXVI. MO TI'S UNIVERSAL LOVE

THE brief and biting comments of Mencius on Mo Ti's doctrine of Universal Love contrast strangely with the ponderous and repetitive presentation of that doctrine in the *Mo Tzŭ Book*. That Mencius should have been able, as apparently he was, to demolish the doctrine with the weapon of scorn suggests that the case made out for it was a weak one, as indeed an analysis of the arguments shows it to have been.

Stripped of their tautology, these were simple enough. The cause of the disorders and disasters in the world—friction and feuds between States and families, shattered loyalties, rogueries of all kinds—was self-love or the desire of the individual to improve his material position at the expense of other people. The remedy for the disease was the removal of its cause: the substitution for the policy of grab—among princes, ministers and private citizens—of the love of one's neighbour as oneself. With a monotony that tends to become exhausting, " Master Mo, the philosopher " pleads and reiterates that men should go all out for this principle: intrinsically a good one, the fruits of which are good—the feeding of the hungry, the clothing of the naked, the nursing of the sick and the burying of the dead. And because the principle is good (so the reasoning runs) it must be capable of practical application; if there be any doubt on the point, the ancient records provide the necessary proof, for did not the sage-kings (the Great Yü especially) exemplify it in their government?[1] Moreover, the principle is a natural one. What soldier facing the perils of war, or envoy the uncertainties of a distant mission, would not rather entrust his

[1] See Note I.

family to a supporter of this selfless love than to an opponent of it? What people, looking for a ruler in times of plague or famine, would not make a similar choice?

But the principle is recommended, not so much on account of its goodness and naturalness, as on the ground that the exercise of it " pays ". The practitioner of filial piety, who extends this duty to include other people's parents, is promised a dividend in the form of reciprocal attention by the latter to his own parents. It is further intimated that the social obligations generally, if universalized, will operate in this way, yielding a return to the community in benefits of greater safety, more creature comforts. " Master Mo ", who was a utilitarian at heart, seems not to have minded debasing his lofty ethic by linking it with the prospect of gain; nor to have realized that the effect of so doing was to encourage the self-love which he condemned. It escaped him, too, that it was incompatible with the high purposes of Universal Love to suggest imposing it by means of rewards and penalties.

It may be assumed that Mencius (who hated and went about denouncing the profit-motive) was fully alive to the weaknesses in all this argument. But he chose, according to the *Book of Mencius*, to direct his criticism to a single point—that at which the argument threatened to disrupt the Confucian pattern of the social obligations. It was essential to that pattern that the social " good feelings " should be brought to bear on their proper objects; that the feeling of filial piety, for instance, should be concentrated on a man's own family. Mo Ti himself and the moderates of Mohism professed anxiety to preserve these good feelings, and asserted that Universal Love, if allowed free play, would strengthen and improve them. But it was intolerable to Mencius that this kind of love should be given priority over the precious obligations; still more so that it should be regarded (by advanced Mohists) as entirely subsuming them. In that extreme form it was clearly impracticable, for (as Mencius pointed out to one such Mohist) man's instincts were against "loving all men equally"; in any case it was subversive of filial piety, and for that reason, if for no other, a determined effort had to be made to destroy it. Of the weapons available to him that of ridicule commended itself to Mencius as the best for the purpose.

It may seem surprising, after all this, to find Confucius in the *Chuang Tzŭ Book* represented as identifying—supposedly to Lao Tzŭ—the great Confucian virtues of *jên* and *i* with "universal love", and being blamed by Lao Tzŭ for thrusting them in that form upon the world. But the accusation was not so much a falsity as a distortion of the facts. For, while love in the Confucian sense was "graded" so as to operate intensively within a special area,[1] it was the intention, indeed the command, of the Master that it should go out in a modified degree to all men everywhere. A young man's duty, he says in the *Analects*, is to satisfy the demands of filial piety and, when this has been done, to have charitable feelings towards everyone. Again, there is the much-quoted citation of the disciple Tzŭ Hsia in the same work: "To a gentleman all within the Four Seas are his brothers." *Jên* likewise, as Confucius conceived it, was unlimited in scope; he rarely gave anything approaching a definition of it, but once, when he did so, he generalized it as "Love towards men".[2]

[1] Covering the "Five Relationships" between men (sovereign and subject, father and son, husband and wife, old and young, and friend and friend).

[2] The Golden Rule or "Way of the Measuring Square" in Confucianism (see Note XI) was in terms as all-embracing as Mohist Universal Love. Fundamentally, the two conceptions differed from each other hardly at all.

Universal Love in the sense of a real, far-reaching, but essentially residual, warmth of regard was as much a part of Mencius' teaching as of his Master's. And the former, as if to underline Mo Ti's "perversion" of Universal Love, carried the Confucian "grading" further and prescribed an inferior form of "solicitude for animals".

XXVII. A CHAPTER ON MUSIC

It is clear from the *Analects* and other sources that Confucius was deeply interested in music, both the music of the ancients and that of his own time. It is clear also that this interest of his was twofold: that he not only loved music as such, but regarded it as a valuable, indeed an indispensable, accessory of the moral life. In Ssŭ-ma Ch'ien's biography he is depicted as an eager and apt student of music, which he practised both instrumentally and vocally; he appears, too, as a teacher of the subject, and his technical proficiency must have been considerable, or he could not have reformed (as a saying of his suggests he did) the music of his native State of Lu. There is evidence in the *Analects* of a distinction in his mind between aesthetic and ethical qualities in music; thus the music of peace associated with Shun, which he described as " perfectly beautiful and perfectly good ",[1] he preferred to the martial music of Wu, which though " perfectly beautiful " was not " perfectly good ". As to the place of music in the moral life, he ranked it as a third great instrumentality (the other two being poetry and ritual) by means of which the " finish " is given to that life. But the references to music in the *Analects*, though fairly numerous, are scattered and disjointed; those in *Mencius* are few and philosophically unilluminating; and elsewhere in the Four Books there is an almost unbroken silence on the subject.

---

[1] It is recorded of him that, after listening on one occasion to the music of Shun, he was so affected by it as to become " oblivious to the taste of his food for three months ". In contrast to this, he condemned as " licentious " the music that went with certain of the ancient ballads (the " songs of Chêng " in the *Book of Poetry*).

The Classics of Confucianism, as distinct from the Four Books, amply make up for this deficiency in the latter. The ancient writings available to Confucius, which constituted the basis and background of his teaching, included a *Book of Music*,[1] which has not survived; but the formal and elaborate treatise on music, which stands incorporated in the classical *Book of Rites*, leaves no doubt as to the ideas of his school on this topic. The main theme of the author of this treatise (justly called by Sir R. F. Johnston " one of the most fascinating documents in the language ") is the potency of the right kind of music as an instrument of good government.

On the basis that music is a product of the mind and depends for its character on the various emotions which, actuated from without, agitate the mind, he proceeds to show how the sovereigns of old were careful to control the outward things that affected the minds of their people and consequently their music. It is possible, he asserts, to tell from its music whether politically a State is sound or otherwise; thus the jangling of the " five notes of the scale " in the popular tunes of Chêng and Wei betokens disorder or decadence in those States. Music, he explains, is not mere sound or a combination of sounds but an art, the inner meaning and purpose of which can be apprehended only by " gentlemen "; its true function is, not to give pleasure, but to regulate the movements of the mind and bring out the essential goodness of man's nature.

In a comparative study of music and ritual the author pronounces the former to be something internal, which unifies and composes the operations of the mind; ritual, on the other hand, is external, its method being differentiation (as shown, for example, in the gradations of social rank). But the achievement of the two agencies is the same—the creation of harmony; in

[1] See Note XXVIII.

the first case a harmony of mind, in the second of manners. And this harmony, at the highest levels of music and ritual, is identical with the harmony of Nature (of " heaven and earth ") ; and out of it come great virtues—in particular, kindly sympathy (*jên*) and rightness (*i*). As music (with its accompaniment of miming and dances) reflects the unity of the visible heaven, so ritual (with its dressings-up and posturings) is patterned on the diverse processes of the visible earth.

The parallelism with Nature is made more specific by linking to *jên*, with its affinity to music, the activities of growth and ripening in spring and summer ; and to *i*, with its affinity to ritual, the corresponding phenomena of autumn and winter. In all this analysis music and ritual are given not only a cosmic but a mystical significance. Described as co-equal with the world of experience, these two great complementary powers nevertheless transcend the limits of that world and join company with Goodness itself.

Reverting to the subject of government, the author recalls the musical systems of Shun (" the inventor of the five-stringed lute ") and other sage-rulers of the past, under which heads of the feudal states were allowed to perform the imperial music as a reward for virtuous conduct and sound administration. Assisted in this way, those heads were encouraged to improve themselves still further, and—such being the force of example —the people under their charge advanced in virtue. Incidentally, the author notes, the beneficent influence of the music, coupled with the restraints of the ritual, served to prevent drunkenness and other excesses at gatherings of the people on special occasions.

The methods by which the sage-rulers made music an institution are explained in detail : how, aiming to convey through the medium of music ideas that would elevate the hearts of their people, they reformed its technique, decreed it a subject of education and established schools in which it should be taught. Again and again the author insists on the sensitiveness of the human mind to the impressions of music, and stresses the potential value (for purposes of government) of its ready response to the right kind of music. An almost lyrical description of what the "five notes" can accomplish, if properly handled, leads to the much-quoted pronouncement, which contains the purport of the whole treatise, that "virtue is the tough stem of man's nature, and music is its flowering".

The rest of the work is largely taken up with reported discussions ; on, for instance, the respective merits of the old and new styles of music, and the meaning of various movements in the pantomimes of Wu. But the praise of music generally is continued, and it reaches a climax in a remarkable passage, which deals with the power of music in the hands of a sage. To music, as managed by that superlative agent, the author attributes an influence over Nature itself ; so that birds, beasts, plants, trees—all things, in fact, in the natural order—are given an impetus to grow and mature and prosper.[1]

It is impossible to be sure how far Confucius would have endorsed in detail the sentiments expressed in this treatise. Conceivably he would have regarded some of its higher flights as extravagant. It is clear that music meant much more to him than "a mere sounding of bells and drums", but how much more it is difficult, on the evidence of his recorded utterances, to determine.

---

[1] This touches the ancient Chinese conception of "Heaven, Earth and Man" as a trinity, and is comparable with a passage in the *Doctrine of the Mean*, where the "perfectly genuine man" is credited with a capacity for forwarding the creative work of Nature.

XXVIII. "THE HUNDRED SCHOOLS"

PERHAPS the most remarkable feature of the mixed collection of Taoist writings, which survives under the "umbrella" name of *Chuang Tzŭ*, is the contrast between the concluding essay and the thirty-two others that precede it. While those who compiled the earlier essays followed in the main the method of poetry and used, in speaking of rival schools, the voice of a not too scrupulous advocacy, the author of the thirty-third stands out as a true philosopher-critic, whose method is the scientific one and whose subject—the purest form of Taoism and various historical departures from it—is handled with a high degree of steadiness and poise. The standard by which the so-called "Hundred Schools" are tested by this writer is the familiar "Way of the Ancients"[1]; that perfect life in an impossible golden age, on which the Taoists harped continually. What is new and interesting about him is that he discards the usual weapons of controversy (ridicule, faint praise and so on) and deals judicially with the schools that he surveys; admitting and giving weight to their merits so that the adverse judgment, when he comes to pass it finally, is felt to have been justly reached.

Thus in the opening section, where Confucianism is touched on, he seems to give a qualified approval to the make-up of the Confucian "gentleman", even mentioning ritual and music (on which Taoists as a rule frowned severely) in a favourable sense without any sign of reprobation. He goes on, moreover,

---

[1] One section, the fifth, of the thirty-third essay is devoted to praise of two of these ancients: Lao Tan (Lao Tzŭ) the central figure of Taoism, and the "warden of the pass" at whose instance Lao Tzŭ was said to have written the *Tao Tê Ching*.

to recommend, as repositories of the lore of the ancients, the books of *Poetry, History, Ritual, Music, Changes* and the *Spring and Autumn Annals* ; books on which what he calls " the scholars of Tsou and Lu " (the birthplaces respectively of Mencius and Confucius) based their teaching. It is clear from what follows, however, that he regarded Confucianism as a disruptive influence, an example of fatal branching into " schools " of the one great primitive stump of Taoist truth.

On the subject of Mohism he is more expansive, and in the course of a penetrating study of this movement picks out for special criticism Mo Ti's condemnation of music and insistence on rigid simplicity in funeral arrangements. Austerity in these matters, he argues, is all very well up to a point and the pursuit of it is to be found in the " Way of the Ancients " ; but the enjoyment of music and ritual in moderation is natural to men, and it is overdoing austerity to seek, as Mo Ti did, to deprive them of that enjoyment. After blaming Mo and his followers for modelling themselves on the Great Yü and " wearing the hair off their legs " in mistaken efforts to benefit society, he dilates on the splitting of Mohism into schools, each with its own leader and all wrangling together interminably over doctrine and logic. Yet in spite of all this he generously allows that, while Mo Ti's practice was wrong, his theory was right ; and that his system, if not conducive to good government, was at least calculated to produce something better than disorder. And then, as though the fair-mindedness of the critic had not gone far enough, he pays Mo Ti the high compliment of being " one of the finest men in the world, decrepit from overwork perhaps, but not to be disregarded—a true gentleman."

The Taoists disliked " clever " people, and the dialectical ingenuities of Hui Shih and his school of " sophists " drew from the author of the thirty-third essay some pungent yet balanced criticism. He refers derisively to Hui Shih's prowess in debate and showmanship as a rhetorician, to his tricks of logic and " gnat-like evolutions ", to his travelling equipment of " five cartloads of books ". But he is careful to support his strictures with evidence and quotes a number of Hui Shih's riddles or paradoxes to show " how narrow was his way ". And while he charges him with chasing only fugitive things and achieving nothing of real value, he concedes to him the possession of " very great gifts ".

The section which deals with Chuang Tzŭ as a Taoist in the succession from Lao Tzŭ is, as might have been expected, altogether laudatory. But it is a model of compactness and comprehensiveness and is substantially true as a summary of his outstanding attributes—his soaring and exuberant imagination, his originality as a thinker, his grasp of fundamentals, his power of communicating mysteries, and his mastery of the literary art.

XXIX. MOHIST ICONOCLASM

In criticizing the founder of Mohism for condemning music and elaborate funerals, the Taoist commentator on "The Hundred Schools" was acting, perhaps unconsciously, as a defender of the Confucians. For it was to the latter that Mo Ti's strictures on these topics were directed, and though only the externals of Confucianism were in question, his attack on them is significant of much in the Mohist outlook.

The character of Mo Ti seems to have had in it something stark and even stern, and there is a certain primitive ruggedness about his doctrines. The universal love which he advocated was a simpler thing than the graded love of the Confucians, and the keynote of the practical rules laid down by him for the conduct of life was austerity. What shocked him specially in the disordered conditions of his time was the luxurious living of the highly placed, and holding (as the Confucians also did [1]) that it was no use teaching morality to the masses until their physical needs had been met, he pressed for retrenchment and a re-direction of productive activity as a step towards this end. His formula for this in effect was a sufficiency for all; and by a sufficiency he meant just that—food, clothing and shelter that satisfied the primary wants but stopped short of indulgence.

The task of providing this common sufficiency, as Mo Ti saw it, was a formidable one, demanding a concentration of available

[1] Thus, Confucius told a disciple of his that the first thing to be done for a multitudinous population was to enrich it; the next thing, he said, was to instruct it. So also Mencius pleaded for a proper standard of living for the common people; without such a standard, he argued, they could not acquire the "fixed heart" necessary for the reception of moral teaching.

energy. He therefore added, as a corollary to his rule of frugality, a rule of hard work for all ; and he seems in this connection to have expected a special effort from four classes : heads of government, officials, farmers and women. Opponents of Mohism (particularly the Taoists) were pleased to accentuate the peculiarities of its adherents—their bustling activity, their workmanlike garments, the utilitarian pattern of the shoes they wore. But if in fact they " rubbed the hair off their legs " in devoted service to society, they had the highest possible sanction in antiquity for doing so ; for did not the Great Yü, their chosen patron, in an age of greater simplicity, exert himself over the flood-waters in this very way ?

So firmly set was Mo Ti on achieving a standard of decent living for the masses, that he would tolerate nothing, however innocent in itself, that did not directly serve that all-important practical purpose. The refinements of culture—the arts and elegant crafts—he rejected as failing to satisfy this test ; and he singled out for special condemnation the art and cult of music, which he viewed as a gross example of non-productiveness and an utter waste of time and money.[1] In the multiform edifice of Confucian philosophy music was a pillar, or perhaps rather a buttress, contributing to its stability and strength ; and in condemning music Mo Ti was striking a blow at Confucianism that was calculated to be most damaging. But the contest in this matter was an unequal one ; as the commentator on " The Hundred Schools " remarked, the nature of man demanded music, and the advantage obviously lay with the side whose plan it was to exploit this demand, and not with that which sought to repress it.

[1] Included in this condemnation were the mimings, dances and paraphernalia of costumes and " properties ", that went with the music. The performances at court were paid for out of public funds.

Mo Ti could have argued similarly and with equal force against any of the forms of ritual, the grand concomitant of music in the Confucian system; in actual fact he seems to have been preoccupied with funeral and mourning forms and to have made these his chief target in this field. It was nothing new for the Confucians to be charged with turning burial occasions into costly parades and elaborating the expressions of grief unduly; the Master himself, his biographer records, was so charged by jealous enemies in his lifetime. The novelty, when Mo Ti brought these charges, was the employment by him as a weapon of the method of logic; and there can be no doubt that his substitution of reasoned argument for mere denunciation added to the effectiveness of the attack. But the spectacle of two great schools of thought at issue over the thickness of coffin wood, the quality and size of shrouds and the depth of graves, could hardly be considered an edifying one.

The significance of the Mohist iconoclasm is that it represented a serious and planned attempt—the first of its kind—to check the tendency of the Confucians to over-ornament the actions of life and the circumstances of death. It is of interest as marking an early phase of the age-long conflict between the ritualist and the puritan.

XXX. IDEAS ABOUT WAR

In a survey of warfare in China from the earliest times, the author of the *Huai-nan Tzŭ Book*, who as a Taoist must have hated all war, found that even offensive war was justified if it were waged for a sound ethical purpose. In illustration of this he cited the sage-kings of remote antiquity, whose constant fighting had always a desirable end—the suppression of a tyrant, the quelling of a revolt. Such fighting, he held, was no more reprehensible than " combing the hair or hoeing up weeds from the ground ". But for purely aggressive or acquisitive war this writer had nothing but condemnation, and he had only to mention Chieh and Chou, the classic examples of bad kingship, to demonstrate how military force should not be used.

While there was some common ground between the Taoists and the Confucians, and some between each of these groups and the Mohists, a few leading ideas are to be found in all three ; among these was the general theory of war propounded in the above-mentioned survey of *Huai-nan Tzŭ*. Thus Mencius, Mo Ti and the Taoist sage were at one in regarding all war as a lamentable thing, and each in his own way expatiated on the madness of war and the havoc and misery caused by it. So, too, the three schools were prepared to condone the types of war that could be classed as defensive or punitive. In the *Tao Tê Ching*, where such war is accepted with grief as an unavoidable necessity, the commander of troops is given instructions how to govern himself (Taoistically) in battle and after it. In *Mencius* the head of a small State, menaced by powerful neighbouring States, is advised by the " Second Sage " to look to his moats and walls and the manning of his defences ; and elsewhere in the same book the punitive expeditions, eleven in number, of T'ang, the great sage-emperor, are referred to with approval. And in the *Mo Tzŭ Book*, the collected writings of the Mohist purveyors of "universal love", a whole section is devoted to practical measures for the defence of cities, including the use of ingenious engines of war.

The three schools also spoke, or rather shouted, with a single voice in vehement denunciation of aggressive war. It is not enough to say, however, that their findings on this subject were unanimous; it must be noted that the respective arguments on which those findings rested differed widely.

The ideal of Mohism was universal love, and aggressive warfare was the very antithesis of that. But the argument deployed against it was mainly the utilitarian one: that the fruits of conquest—the material gains—were more than offset by the losses represented by devastated fields and depopulated towns. The heart of Mo Ti doubtless bled for the sufferings of the soldiers and the sorrows of the bereaved, but his interest, the interest of his practical mind, lay in the political and economic effects—the dislocation of government and the setbacks to agriculture and industry, caused by the diversion of manpower to the business of war.

In Taoism a fundamental principle was overcoming by yielding, as illustrated by the "actionless action" of water, the weak and unresisting element, which by-passes the opposing rock, yet wears it down in the process and finally masters it. It was from this particular angle—the supremacy of unassertiveness, of gentleness—that Taoist doctors looked at war and denounced [1] the use of weapons ("ill-omened things") on behalf of any

---

[1] As in the thirty-first chapter of the *Tao Tê Ching*. The authors of the *Chuang Tzŭ* and *Lieh Tzŭ Books*, though wholly opposed to violence as such, are strangely silent on the theme of war.

aggressive cause. Between the exponent of quietism and the warmonger there could be no parley or compromise whatever, for the spirit of militarism was the negation of *tê*, the magical-moral transforming power of Tao.

The essence of the case against wars of aggression, as advanced by Mencius,[1] was that they imperilled *jên* and *i*, the supporting pillars of the citadel of Confucian morality. At a meeting with the itinerant philosopher, Sung Tzŭ, an advocate of pacifism and a militant one, Mencius applauded his aim but rejected his argument that war " did not pay ", and urged him to argue on the basis of *jên* and *i*. The idea of judging a course of action by reference to its profitableness was repugnant to Mencius ; the only test he was willing to apply was whether it conformed to kindliness and justice, and it was self-evident that wanton violence, political or private, could not possibly do that.

The common attitude of these scholars towards war, thus based on the differentiated logic of their schools, doubtless represented to some extent a reaction against the troubled conditions of the times. It was natural for the philosophic mind to recoil from the bloody bickerings of the feudal lords, which seemed to have no intermission and no end. There was one dissentient group—the Legalists—who adopted war as an instrument of policy, but Legalism and all that it implied were contrary to the instinct of the Chinese people, and its gospel of force could not survive for long. " The Chinese ", Dr. Lin Yutang has said, " hate war and will always hate war."

[1] Confucius seems not to have interested himself in the ethics of war, and no important pronouncement by him on the subject is recorded.

XXXI. THE BLOCK AND THE CHISEL

In their search for symbols to illustrate their teachings the Taoist and Confucian philosophers sometimes hit upon the same image (that of water, for example) and then proceeded to develop it in their different ways. At other times they exercised their choice independently, and rival images resulted; thus the Taoists adopted for a symbol the block that no carver's hand had touched, and the Confucians the cutting and finishing processes employed by a carver in working up his material.

In the ancient *Book of Poetry*, from which the great Confucians delighted to quote, a certain prince of Wei was praised for being " cut and filed, chiselled and polished ". It is not clear whether the poet was referring to ethical or aesthetic qualities, but in the *Analects* the disciple Tzŭ Kung, having interpreted the phrase in a moral sense, is promptly commended by Confucius for his understanding of the poetry. In the *Great Learning*, where the same phrase is cited with its context, the meaning is explained: the cutting and filing are the processes of learning, the chiselling and polishing those of cultivation of the self. Learning and self-culture, self-culture through learning —such was the high course advocated in the *Great Learning*. A lengthy business and a laborious one, this shaping and refining of moral personality; and as emblems of it how apt were the operations of the worker in ivory, the sculptor of jade!

" The Way (of the Mean) is not far from men; it is indeed nearer to them—to borrow an analogy from the *Book of Poetry* —than the pattern of an axe-handle is to the block of wood from which a new axe-handle is to be fashioned." A saying of Confucius to this effect is recorded in the *Doctrine of the Mean*.

The poem referred to was connected by tradition with that master of moral accomplishments, the Duke of Chou, and the point of the saying would seem to be that the ordinary person —the unwrought block—is by nature a potential Duke of Chou and needs only the transforming power of "The Way" to raise him to the level of that ideal figure. For the purpose of effecting this transformation a sure and sufficient instrument was available —the instrument of "learning", that is, study of the moral principles, the ritual and the music of the ancients. In the use of this instrument to chip and trim the roughnesses and angularities of man's moral self lay the whole meaning of education in the Confucian sense.[1]

Roughness and angularity: from the Taoist standpoint it was all wrong to depreciate these qualities. It was a question of conserving or, if lost, of recovering them, for did they not stand for Primitive Simplicity, of which virgin timber with all its natural irregularities of form was a perfect symbol? In the *Tao Tê Ching* the ancients of Taoism are stated to have been "like timber in the rough", and those to whom the book was addressed are exhorted to "return to the state of the unwrought block". In that state of freedom from all preoccupation there was no room for self-culture through learning; true knowledge, according to Taoist ideas, was only to be had intuitively from within, and viewed from this angle Confucian "chiselling", and all that it implied, ceased to have any relevance at all.[2]

[1] At the outset of the Treatise on Education in the *Book of Rites* a comparison is made between the cutting of jade into objects of art and the formation of character by "learning".

[2] All this is echoed in the *Chuang Tzŭ Book*, which emphasizes that any "shaping" of the self must be entirely undeliberate like Tao itself.

XXXII. THE TWO "TAOS"

AMONG the anti-Confucian anecdotes, that were a prominent feature of Taoist propaganda, there is one (associated with the philosopher Yang Chu, whose peculiar views were basically Taoist) in which followers of Confucius are compared to a party of people searching for a lost sheep, who themselves get lost in a maze of paths and by-paths. The Taoists saw a special danger in multiple approaches, such as the Confucians favoured, to the citadel of Truth; for pathways of doctrine (if there were more than one) tended to branch into lesser tracks with serious consequences to orthodoxy and discipline of thought.[1] In the Yang Chu anecdote a case is quoted of three pupils of the Confucian school, who, after having studied *jên* and *i* together under the same master, wholly disagreed among themselves as to what these much-vaunted virtues meant.

The "Tao" of the Confucians was repugnant to the Taoists because, instead of being one and indivisible, it was a complex of many modes or "ways"; to the Confucians, on the contrary, it seemed for that very reason a mighty, a many-splendoured thing. The Taoists might talk about "all being one" in the unity of "Tao", as they understood that term; but the actual world, that of living men, was fretted with differences, deep-cut and ineradicable—natural differences of character and capacity, differences of relative position involved in the immemorial set-up of society. How impractical it would be in such a world to prescribe a uniform course for all to walk in! The young

---

[1] The same point is made in the *Tao Tê Ching*, where the author says: "The Great Highway (of the Taoists) is plain and easy; but men prefer the by-paths (of the Confucians)."

person, the ordinary man, the "scholar and gentleman", the minister, the prince—as the Confucian trainer in morals saw them, each of these was a separate "case", demanding specialized treatment within the general framework of the ethical scheme. But inevitably the "cases" tended to coalesce; it was imperative, for instance, that the prince should be a "gentleman", and the duties of a filial son were incumbent on them both. The sets of rules for particular individuals overlapped one another, therefore, to a considerable extent; and, notwithstanding the labels attached to them, these "private" ways (the "Way of a Ruler", the "Way of a Gentleman" and the rest) were in essence and direction the same Way—that of the Virtues, especially of *i* and *li* and *chih*, with *jên* shining at the end. The Taoists were right, however, in saying that it was dangerous to multiply the aspects of Truth; the over-specialization in later Confucianism of the "Way of a Filial Son" was positive evidence of that.

In the *Tao Tê Ching*, the "bible" of the Taoists, the motion or procedure of "Tao" is stated to be one of returning, of "going home". In its primary and predominant sense in Taoism, that of the principle of Spontaneity in all things, "Tao" was attributeless and therefore could have no procedure; but in the sense of "Nature", the manifestation of that principle, "Tao" was a process, that of spontaneous production, and had motion, that of "dying down to the root".[1] In addition, "Tao" had an ethical meaning—the mode of conduct and thought for a Taoist—and this, correspondingly, was regressive: a path in reverse. It was folly for the Confucians to envisage *ahead of them* a city of man-made values in morals and the arts; to suppose that contentment of mind was to be got by garnishing with so-called graces the original self. Were they blind, not to

[1] That is, returning to "Tao" in its abstract, absolute sense.

see that return to the life of the hamlet was the only hope for mankind ; that simplicity, emptiness, ceasing from effort were the clues to self-realization, and that these lay *behind* ? Confucius seems not to have wanted to challenge this utter inversion of what he regarded as " The Way " [1] ; perhaps he thought it too fanciful to take seriously, or so abstruse and lacking in popular appeal that a planned attack on it was not worth while. There are signs, indeed, in the Four Books (particularly in *Mencius* and the *Doctrine of the Mean*) of a toying by the great Confucians with ideas that properly belonged to the " Tao " of the Taoists ; the rival schools had a common borderland of thought in connection with the concept of " the sage ", and even Taoist " inaction " was invoked by the Confucians to reinforce their teaching on this subject.[2]

But, generally speaking, the two " Taos " [3] were independent of each other and irreconcilable. Pointing, as they did, in opposite directions, they proceeded on widely separated lines, which, however, like the parallel lines of the mathematician, met (so to speak) at infinity.

[1] He did, however, on a famous occasion condemn withdrawal from the world of men as practised by two Taoist recluses whom he met.

[2] See Notes XXIV and XXXIII.

[3] It is not to be supposed that the word " Tao "—an ancient one with a variety of meanings—was the exclusive possession of the Confucian and Taoist schools. Every school of philosophy had its " Tao ", its method of management of life for the purpose of attaining its ideal of Goodness.

XXXIII. THE TAOISM OF TZŬ SSŬ

It has already been remarked,[1] in connection with a saying of Confucius about the government of Shun, that at their highest level—the level of "the sage"—the ideas of Confucianism and Taoism tended to converge. This phenomenon is specially noticeable in the *Doctrine of the Mean*, the work ascribed to Tzŭ Ssŭ, where much attention is given to the characteristics of the sage-ruler as the embodiment of heavenly *ch'êng* or perfect genuineness.

In what, from the philosophical standpoint, may be regarded as the pivotal passage of this work, a distinction is drawn between acquired genuineness, which is all that the ordinary man can hope for, and intuitive genuineness, which is the possession and prerogative of the sage. In the former case the path laid down for man's following is a typically Confucian one—widespread, intensive and unremitting study, and practice, of what is good. But in the second case there is no question of a path or a journey, for the sage has "arrived"; and as a master of heavenly *ch'êng* he hits what is right naturally, without deliberation or effort. It was spontaneity that Taoism predicated of the sage, and the mind of Tzŭ Ssŭ, in thus attributing naturalness to him, was moving on Taoist lines.

A further instance, and a remarkable one, of Taoist proclivities in the thought of Tzŭ Ssŭ is the reference he makes, at the close of a searching study of effectual genuineness in man, to *wu wei* or mystical inaction, which in Taoism was a distinctive—an all-important—tenet. Having characterized that genuineness as continuous in time and co-equal spatially with the material

[1] See Note X.

world, he deduces that it has no limits (is infinite) and concludes, paradoxically after the Taoist manner, that "though invisible it is to be clearly seen, though motionless it moves things, though *inactive* it achieves its ends". There is nothing in the accepted sayings of Confucius corresponding to this cosmic treatment of genuineness, and the conclusion both in form and substance is un-Confucian. The hand indeed may have been that of Tzŭ Ssŭ, but the voice was the voice of Taoism.

So, too, in the final section of the work, where the author quotes a number of passages from the ancient *Book of Poetry* and comments upon them, the impress of Taoist ideas is clearly discernible: in the emphasis on simplicity in the sage-ruler, on the vanity of reputation and a name, on the immateriality of spiritual power. And the device of paradox, so strongly favoured and frequently overworked by Taoist writers, is again in evidence.

SELECTED WORKS BEARING ON CONFUCIANISM

The Texts of Confucianism, by J. Legge. Sacred Books of the East. Oxford. 1899.
The Analects of Confucius, by Arthur Waley. Allen & Unwin. 1938.
Three Ways of Thought in Ancient China, by Arthur Waley. Allen & Unwin. 1939.
The Great Learning and The Mean-in-action, by E. R. Hughes. Dent. 1942.
The Conduct of Life (" Doctrine of the Mean "), by Ku Hung-Ming. John Murray (Wisdom of the East Series).
Confucius, by E. D. Edwards. Blackie. 1940.
The Political Philosophy of Confucianism, by L. S. Hsü. Routledge. 1932.
China Moulded by Confucius, by Cheng Tien-Hsi. Stevens. 1946.
The Sayings of Confucius, by L. Giles. John Murray (Wisdom of the East Series).
Confucius and Confucianism, by R. Wilhelm. Kegan Paul. 1931.
The Wisdom of Confucius, by Lin Yutang. Modern Library, New York. 1938.
Confucianism and Taoism, by B. S. Bonsall. Epworth Press. 1934.

China, A Short Cultural History, by C. P. Fitzgerald. Cresset Press. 1935.
The Spirit of Chinese Philosophy, by Fung Yu-Lan. Kegan Paul. 1947.
History of Chinese Political Thought during the early Tsin Period, by Liang Chi-Chao. Kegan Paul. 1930.
Chinese Philosophy in Classical Times, by E. R. Hughes. Dent. 1942.
The Book of Mencius (abridged), by L. Giles. John Murray (Wisdom of the East Series).
Mencius, by L. A. Lyall. Longmans, Green. 1932.
Mencius on the Mind, by I. A. Richards. Kegan Paul. 1932.
Motse, The Neglected Rival of Confucius, by Yi-Pao Mei. Probsthain. 1934.

INDEX

Analects, Confucian, 5, 6, 7–8, 10, 11, 13, 15, 16, 17, 18, 19, 21, 22, 23, 24, 26, 27, 28, 29, 30, 34, 35, 37, 38, 39, 40, 41, 45, 49, 63, 65, 78
" Ancients, the ", 1–3, 32, 69, 70
Animals, attitude towards, 45–8, 64

Blind, consideration for the, 41–2
Breathing, control of, 52–3, 56

Changes, Book of, 70
Ch'êng (" sincerity "), 6, 19–20, 83
Chi K'ang Tzŭ (dictator of Lu), 29, 30
Ch'i (" vital force "), 11–12, 55–6
Chieh (king of Hsia), 1, 59, 75
Chih (" wisdom "), 27, 28, 50, 81
Chou, Duke of, 1, 59, 79
Chou dynasty, 1
Chou (king of Shang), 1, 59, 75
Chu Hsi (philosopher), 36, 38
Ch'ü Po Yü (official of Wei), 13
Chuang Tzŭ and *Chuang Tzŭ Book*, 2, 9–10, 13–14, 15, 24, 26, 32–4, 43–4, 46, 47–8, 52, 53, 54–5, 56, 63, 69–71, 76, 79
Compassion, doctrine of, 42, 44, 60
Confucius, 4–10, 11, 13–18, 21, 26, 29–31, 35, 37–42, 45–6, 49, 65, 68, 72, 77, 82

Desires, elimination of, 56

Doctrine of the Mean, 5–6, 16, 19–20, 22, 23, 35, 36, 38, 40, 57, 68, 78, 82, 83–4

Education, meaning of, 79
Example, doctrine of, 29–31

" Fasting of the mind ", 9
Filial piety, 1, 18, 21, 41, 62, 63, 81
" Fixed heart ", the, 72

" Gentleman ", the, 18, 19, 26, 28, 35, 40, 66, 69, 81
Golden Rule, the, 23, 24, 41, 63
Great Learning, 23–5, 35, 36, 41, 78
" Great man ", the, 50, 59–60

History, Book of, 70
Hsia dynasty, 1
Hsing (" mind "), 49
Huai-nan Tzŭ Book, 32, 75
Huang Ti (Yellow Emperor), 2, 32–4
Hui Shih (sophist), 70–1
Human nature, goodness of, 42, 49–51, 55, 66
" Hundred Schools ", the, 69–71, 72

I (" justice "), 19, 27, 28, 50, 54, 63, 67, 77, 80, 81
I Li (ritual book), 46

87

INDEX

Inaction, doctrine of, 21-2, 76, 82, 83-4
Infant, doctrine of the, 16, 49-53, 59

Jên ("kindly sympathy"), 19, 20, 26-8, 38, 50, 54, 63, 67, 77, 80, 81

Kao Tzŭ (philosopher), 12, 54-5
Knowledge, kinds of, 16, 32-3, 37, 79

Lao Tzŭ (Taoist sage), 10, 63, 69, 71
"Learning", meaning of, 15, 35, 37, 79
Legalist School, 77
Li ("good form"), 27, 28, 50, 81
Lieh Tzŭ Book, 2, 30, 32, 43, 48, 53, 76

"Measuring Square, Way of the", 23-5, 41, 63
Meditation, practice of, 35-6
Mencius and *Book of Mencius*, 11-12, 16, 18, 19, 23, 27-8, 29, 38, 41, 42, 46, 49-51, 52, 54-60, 61, 62-3, 64, 65, 72, 75, 77, 82
Mo Ti (Mo Tzŭ) and Mohism, 2, 10, 54, 61-4, 70, 72-4, 75, 76
Music and *Book of Music*, 65-8, 70, 73

"Names", doctrine of, 17-18, 29
Nature, doctrine of following, 43-4, 47-8, 54-5

Old age, respect for, 41-2, 59

Poetry, Book of, 65, 70, 78-9, 84
Poverty, views on, 59-60

Reciprocity, principle of, 24
Relationships, the Five, 63
Rites, Book of, 66, 70, 79
Ritual, 8, 66-7, 69, 70, 74

"Sage", the, 6, 16, 20, 21-2, 40, 50, 68, 82, 83
Self-culture, 23, 58, 59, 78, 79
Self-examination, 35-6
Senses, cultivation of the, 2-3, 58, 59
Shang Ti ("God"), 39-40
Shang dynasty, 1
Shun (sage-emperor), 1, 2, 21, 30, 31, 33, 40, 56, 59, 65, 67, 83
Simplicity, Primitive, 32, 44, 46, 54, 79
Sophist School, 70
Spring and Autumn Annals, 70
Ssŭ-ma Ch'ien (historian), 4, 5, 6, 15, 17, 45, 47, 65
Sung Tzŭ (philosopher), 77

T'ang (founder of Shang dynasty), 1, 2, 76
"Tao", meanings of, 82
Tao Tê Ching, 2, 22, 32, 47, 52, 53, 55, 69, 75, 76, 79, 80, 81
Taoism, doctrines of, 9-10, 13-14, 15, 22, 24-5, 32-4, 43-4, 47-8, 52-7, 69, 75, 76-7, 79, 80-4
"Taoism", use of term, 2
Tê ("moral power"), 23, 24, 77
T'ien ("heaven"), 40
Tsêng Tzŭ (disciple of Confucius), 35
Tzŭ Ssŭ (grandson of Confucius), 6, 19-20, 36, 83-4

Universal Love, doctrine of, 2, 54, 61–4, 72, 76
"Unmoved mind", the, 11–12, 55

Virtues, the Four Great, 27–8, 50, 58, 81

War, views on, 75–7
Water as a symbol, 47, 55, 76, 78
"Way of a Gentleman", 6, 38, 81
"Way, the", 12, 78–9, 80–2
Wên (king of Chou), 1, 2
Wu (king of Chou), 1, 2, 65, 68

Wu wei ("inaction"), 21–2, 76, 82, 83–4

Yang Chu (philosopher), 2–3, 54, 58–60, 80
Yao (sage-emperor), 1, 2, 30, 31, 33, 40
Yellow Emperor (Huang Ti), 2, 32–4
Yen Hui (disciple of Confucius), 15–16, 27, 60
Yü the Great (founder of Hsia dynasty), 1, 2, 21, 34, 40, 56, 59, 61, 70, 73